IMAGES OF WALES

CANTON

BRYAN JONES

TEMPUS

First published 1995
New Edition 2003

Tempus Publishing Limited
The Mill, Brimscombe Port,
Stroud, Gloucestershire, GL5 2QG

British Library Cataloguing in Publication Data.
A catalogue record for this book is available from the British Library.

ISBN 0 7524 3010 6

Typesetting and origination by Tempus Publishing Limited
Printed in Great Britain by Midway Colour Print, Wiltshire

IMAGES OF WALES

CANTON

Contents

Foreword

Canton will always have a special place in my affections. It was in the home of Mr & Mrs O'Dare (who kept a café right next to the railway line by Ninian Park) that it was first proposed that I should become the Prospective Labour Parliamentary Candidate for Cardiff Central. The Canton Ward was therefore the beginning of my public life in Cardiff.

Canton is one of the most historic parts of our great capital City. Throughout my thirty-eight and a half years as a Cardiff Member of Parliament in the House of Commons, I regarded Canton as the centre of the Constituency.

Bryan Jones puts the whole City of Cardiff in his debt by his conscientious research, which has resulted in this superb collection of pictures. He brings the history of Canton to life, and I hope that every household in the City will be the proud possessor of this book. His fascination and love for the history of Canton cries out to us on every page. Because I also love Canton and its proud people, I can recommend this new wide-ranging publication without the slightest reserve.

George Thomas
Speaker, House of Commons 1976-1983
Right Honourable The Viscount Tonypandy PC, (Hon) DCL

George Thomas became a teacher in Cardiff until he was adopted as the Cardiff Central Labour candidate in 1946 (the constituency was renamed Cardiff West in 1950). He was Secretary of State for Wales 1968-70, Speaker of the House of Commons 1976-83, and Vice-President of the Methodist Conference 1959-60.

one

Canton: An Introduction

When commissioners came to assess Canton for the Parliamentary Boundaries Review needed for the Reform Bill of 1832 they found a small, sleepy hamlet of two roads and three lanes. This was home for some two hundred folk who lived in fifty or so cottages mostly clustered around the manor house, mill, tithe barn and common of medieval times. It was a place of fields and streams, of orchards and of farms – and of sheep in their thousands, which for centuries had provided a livelihood for most of those who had made the area their home. Rhys the Weaver, for example, was working in his cottage on the edge of the common (Tŷ Rhys y Gwŷdd). So it had been for some six hundred years and so it would continue to be, as far as the commissioners could see.

They were wrong, of course. Within three years the young Queen Victoria had come to the throne and by the time of her death Canton had become a township of forty thousand people. And Rhys the Weaver had taken to running 'Canton Factory' to make up his cloth. The transformation would have astonished the Commissioners, but then Canton has often come as something of a surprise, as has Cardiff itself. This was aptly put by Dr James Mullin, the 'Canton Poet' as he styled himself, tongue-in-cheek. His lines Cardiff described by a person who had never seen it, written around the turn of the century, were prefaced with the words: 'According to some reports, Cardiff is a dirty, dingy, coal producing town somewhere in Wales'. Two of the verses read:

Well, speaking of Cardiff I haven't been there,
But, of course, it is easy to picture the place –
There's nothing about it that's lovely or rare
And the grime of the coal is all over its face
'Tis there you would choke
with the smut and the smoke
And feel yourself held in chaotic embrace.

Its suburbs are surely a desolate scene,
For the volumes of smoke and the showers of
    soot
Have blasted and blackened all, all that is green
And left the whole landscape as black as your
    boot,
With hardly a scrap
That a locust could snap
And never a bite for a four-footed brute.

Just how wrong those ideas were can be seen in many of the photographs that follow.

The development of Canton is outlined here in a sequence of five sections, each of which covers a period in its history. The first (1850-1875) looks at the foundation of modern Canton; the second (1875-1900) at its period of greatest growth, when it was incorporated in the Borough of Cardiff; the third (1900-1914) at its hey-day; the fourth (1914-1939) at the period which includes what has been called the 'Ordeal'; and the fifth, and last, at the Second World War and the recovery from it until 1960. But first it is worth looking at some of the earlier episodes in the story, which take us back to the dawn of our nation. Finally, it should be said that this book is intended to be the first of two parts, so that anything you are expecting to find which is missing has surely a place in volume two.

The history of most localities is moulded more than we realise by where they are, and Canton is no exception. A blend of common sense, historical precedent and common usage defines Canton as lying between the Cardiff and Ely bridges, and reaching southwards from Pencisely Road to the area around Ninian Park. So Canton (Treganna) occupies an area of almost two square miles sandwiched between the River Taff (Afon Tâf) on the east and the River Ely (Afon Elaí) on the west. The map on page 11 indicates that when it was drawn – and probably for 'time out of mind' before then – the hamlet also reached down to the coast of the Bristol Channel, and Canton was therefore surrounded by water on three of its four sides. As it is low-lying, marshy ground which has held many pools and streams, water has obviously played a large part in its story, illustrated typically by this photograph of the floods in 1960. The weather here is kinder than the floods suggest, however. Overall, the climate is mild, and drier and sunnier than most other parts of Wales – for example, grapes have been grown in Romilly Road for many years – although a south-westerly prevailing wind makes for changeable conditions. The farming hamlet would have found that the climate favoured grass (the 'wealth of Wales') and indeed 74 per cent of the land was pasture. Corn was also raised, and Canton shared the climate of the Vale which made it 'for corn and good fruits the garden of Wales and for good cattle of all kinds the nursery of the west'. February has the coldest days, although January is the month with the coldest average temperature of 45°F (7.2°C). Spring arrives relatively early and the months of April to October are mostly frost-free. The warmest month is July, with an average temperature of 62°F (16.5°C) and autumn days and nights are warmer than those in spring. Rain falls on average 170 days each year to provide a mean annual rainfall of about 40 inches, with October being the wettest month; snow lies on the ground on an average of four mornings each year. June is the driest month, and the sunniest, and there is often a second dry spell in September which coincides with the corn harvest. The sun shines for an average of 1,500 hours every year and – should you ever need to plot a course – Canton lies at a latitude of 51°28′ N and a longitude of 3°8′ W.

Much the greater part of the land underlying Canton was formed by the rivers Ely and Taff as part of the natural process of building up their 'flood plains' with the mud and silt carried by the rivers from the hills of the coalfield to the north; it is alluvial ground. Under the original conditions when the rivers were more free to wander at will they would have formed meanders but man has caused traces of most of these to disappear. Mid-eighteenth century maps do, however, show a large bend immediately downstream from Cardiff Bridge. This bend, which extended eastwards to St Mary Street, was cut off to straighten the Taff when the South Wales Railway was built through the town. The complementary bends are now hidden under parts of Sophia Gardens and Pontcanna Fields. The only solid rocks near the surface in the area are those of Triassic age which form the ridge which extends from a line just north of Romilly Road – and well seen at Penhill – to form the bank upon which the village of Llandaff stands. The low-lying land of Canton is largely below 30 feet above mean sea level, and the bluff at Penhill rises abruptly to over 80 feet. Amongst these Triassic rocks there is a distinctive layer which provides what is perhaps the most unusual of the local building stones – the Radyr stone. In the days before convenient means of transport became common, the architecture of an area necessarily depended upon whatever local materials were available. In one way this lingered on in Canton where, more than anywhere else in Cardiff, Radyr stone was used. This is a very rough reddish stone, described as a breccia technically and as a 'pudding stone' by builders to denote the inclusion of large distinctive fragments of grey limestone. It was used mainly for capping stones for railway bridges but was also used extensively to provide variety as gate posts, quoins, window sills and parapets in buildings. In a number of the older streets of Canton, large slabs of it – often up to 6 feet long and over 4 feet wide – have been set on edge to form the boundary walls of front gardens (now commonly cemented over). Radyr stone came from a quarry close to the west bank of the Taff, north-west of Llandaff Bridge, and was used from about 1850 until the 1920s. The quarry is shown by the photograph in 1884, when a steam crane with a vertical boiler can be seen at work.

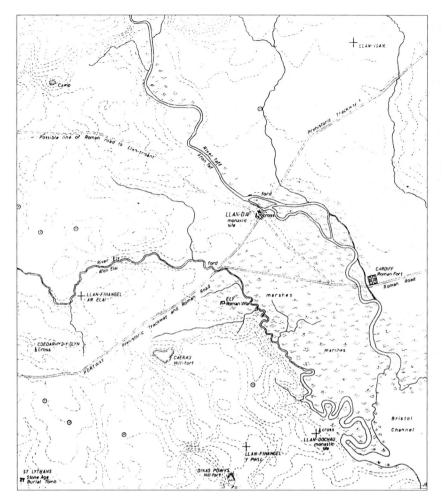

Sometime around 600 BC a party of Bronze-Age raiders from the mountains around Brecon chose this as a good site to launch a foray on the wealthy farmlands of the Cotswolds. They returned in triumph to the spot near Leckwith Bridge (the tidal limit of the Ely) where an archaeologist has described them stopping to bury a portion of their plunder as a thanksgiving to their spirit of the waters. Their hoard was found at a depth of three feet near Ninian Park in 1928 and is now held by the National Museum of Wales. Those raiders were some of the Brythons who gave our land its first name, language and religion, and their presence here takes us back to the dawn of our nation. About seven hundred years later the Romans sought to conquer Wales and suppress opposition from the Druids, whose stronghold was Anglesey. Canton was in the territory of the Silures, whose tenacious resistance moved even the legions' own historian Tacitus to comment admiringly. They are said to have been led for a time by the heroic Caractacus, whose noble speech to the Roman Senate after his capture was once known by every schoolboy, and whose family is claimed to have built the first Christian church in Rome (St Pudentia). The Silures defeated three Roman generals before the Governor, Julius Frontinus, took successful command. It was part of his holding strategy to construct the Via Julia Maritima between Gloucester and Neath, which largely followed an ancient track and more recently became the A48. He then built the first Cowbridge road through Canton as a link between the Via Julia and his fortress at Cardiff. The map is reproduced from *Llandaf Past and Present* by John B. Hilling, and it suggests that Llandaff Road too has Roman origins as a route to Llantrisant.

11

THE OLD BRIDGE EL...

In Canton today we tend to look east towards the town. In the Middle Ages the people here would have looked north to Llandaff, and in the Dark Ages probably south to Dinas Powys. But it is perhaps to the west that we should look for the origins of the hamlet, for in Ely there was one of the Roman villas which all seem to have lain deserted after the legions departed around AD 400. Professor Leslie Alcock has suggested that in the chaos of the Dark Ages the tenants of the villas' farms may have found it unsafe to live in isolated steadings – there is evidence of massacres then – and so they may have come together to form the bond hamlets devoted to mixed farming which were prevalent on the eve of the Norman conquest. It is possible that some of the local tenants of the villa at Ely came together in this way to found the hamlet of Canton sometime between AD 400 and AD 500. More certainly, it is the Dark Ages to which we owe the fact that Canton is one of the handful of places in Britain which have taken their name from a female saint. Can-ton is the 'ton' (or homestead) on the Canna, which was a small stream that rose in Llandaff Fields and flowed through the hamlet to join the Taff below Brook Street. Its name comes from St Canna, who is believed to be the sixth-century daughter of Tewdwr Mawr (of St Tudor's, Mynyddislwyn) and the sister-in-law and disciple of St Illtud, the 'Master of Wales'. She is also said to have been a relative and contemporary of the legendary King Arthur. When Britons came under attack from the four points of the compass and were at their most desperate, Canna and her companions of the Celtic 'Age of Saints' brought them the gospel of peace and hope – and in so doing created Christian Wales. Canna herself founded two churches which remain, at Llan-gan near Bridgend and Llan-gan in Pembrokeshire. She bore St Crallo by her husband St Sadwrn ('Marchog' – the knight) and her son founded his own church at Llangrallo (now Coychurch). After Sadwrn's death she is reputed to have married a Cotswold prince. South Wales, therefore, provides perhaps the only area in Britain where we can visit the churches of saints from three generations of one family. St Canna is commemorated in Canton by the dedication of a chapel in the parish church of St John's and by the Sunday school banner there.

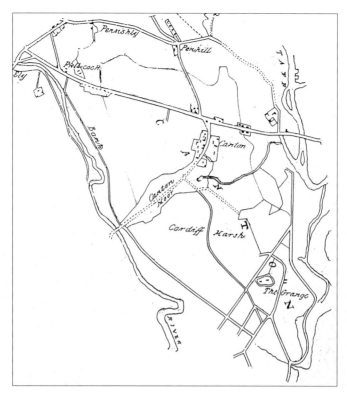

The name of Canton first appears in that of a family who were probably tenants of its manor in the early thirteenth century – Lucia de Kanetune, Nicholas de Kenetone and Richard de Canetone. Many Norman families were given land and encouraged to settle here after the conquest and it was common for them to adopt the name of their new home as their own – as at Roath where its name was taken by an early Roth family. The family here surely did the same, which suggests that Canton was already a well-established name. The hamlet itself is first mentioned later in the same century, as a manor held by the bishop of Llandaff; the land between the rivers Taff and Ely was reputedly granted to the Church by Meurig, king of Glywysing, in the seventh century. The manor emerges in the 1200s complete with manor house (on the northern corner of Atlas Road and Leckwith Road where it remained until this century); a mill (probably on the same site as the mill at the bottom of Bassett Street which also survived until this century); tithe barn and common; and the demesnes which were worked by the serfs of the hamlet. In 1450 the manor, together with that of Llandaff, was purchased by Sir David Mathews, who saved the life of King Edward IV at the Battle of Towton on Palm Sunday in 1461 and was hence created Grand Standard Bearer of All England. He is commemorated in Llandaff Cathedral by a fine tomb, and in Canton by Cae Syr Dafydd of which Thompson's Park formed a part. The manor remained in his family for almost four hundred years until in 1818 it was purchased by Sir Samuel Romilly, a leading law reformer and Solicitor-General. In 1852 it was sold on by Romilly's sons to William Sheward Cartwright. The commons were purchased by the Cardiff Corporation in 1885, who compensated the commoners and undertook to use the land for recreational purposes. The medieval structure of Canton was thus established in the thirteenth century and it remained more or less unaltered until 1850. It is illustrated by the map, which was drawn to accompany the Parliamentary Boundaries Review prior to the Reform Act of 1832. It shows the main cluster of dwellings around the manor house and common, with a smaller group around Kings Castle. Canton Pool, a well-documented feature south-east of the common, can be seen at the tip of a stream leading to a tributary of the Taff.

When Cromwell besieged Cardiff Castle the site he chose for his cannon was near Kings Road: it was the only high ground in the area. This advantage was provided by an ancient raised earthwork mound, still faintly visible in 1921, alongside the Canna stream near the present public house. It was this earthwork which originally bore the name 'Kings Castle' – so called because of its position on the 'king' or bend of the stream – and it raises the question of whether it represents the remains of the original settlement of the hamlet. Certainly the area is one of the oldest inhabited parts of Canton, with a Kings Castle inn recorded there in 1710. The name 'Kings Castle' was also taken by one of Canton's oldest and largest private houses, which stood a little to the east; it is shown in the photograph not long before it was demolished in 1892 to make way for the Memorial Hall. *Cardiff Records* (J. Hobson Matthews, 1898) refers to it as 'an ancient and very solidly built house in the hamlet of Canton' and quotes Mr William Levers as saying that he 'visited the Kings Castle very frequently. Although it had undergone many alterations, it was an old-fashioned house. You went down at least one step to enter the house and you could easily touch the ceiling with your hand'. The house and its occupant featured in a court case of 1696 in which Nicholas Greene blocked a water-course and flooded Cowbridge Road '...designing and wickedly minding not only to vex and oppress Henry Fox in certain ways, but also to bring and put all the liege subjects of our Lord the King that is now going, returning, riding and journeying through and across such highway, in danger to lose their lives...'. Thirty years later another Canton man, James Jenkin, was in court for not paying his tithes. At that time this was a common form of protest by puritans who resented supporting the established Church, and they were much in evidence in Canton. The large congregation of Llandaff Quakers met in Canton Manor House, where they were visited by George Fox.

Leckwith Bridge, 1900. This is the oldest surviving structure in Canton, a listed building hidden behind the viaduct which replaced it in 1934. J. Hobson Matthews declares that it is the oldest bridge in the neighbourhood of Cardiff and says that the hermit Llewellyn ap David placed his hermitage there in the fifteenth century 'it being an appropriate site for the receipt of alms'. John Leland, writing in 1536, describes it as being soundly built of stone. Cardiff Bridge in 1748 is shown below in a section of a panoramic view of Cardiff from the Canton bank of the Taff, in a copper plate engraving by Samuel and Nathaniel Buck. This was one of a series in which the artists sought to create classical views of the major towns in England and Wales.

The renovated cottage at No 4 Romilly Road is said to be the oldest surviving home in Canton and one of the smallest in Cardiff. It was built as a one-up one-down 'tŷ bach twt' not later than 1740. The photograph was taken in the 1930s and shows Violet Young, whose family lived there from 1905 until the 1970s. A neighbour, in her nineties and still living nearby, remembers her part of the road as largely a crocus patch, with cows grazing in the field behind. Romilly Road has an interesting contrast of architecture, one side dating from the turn of the century which had large houses for families with domestic servants, whilst the other has smaller houses built thirty years later when labour-saving appliances were common and families were smaller.

The terrace of thatched cottages in Cathedral Road, 1890s, on the north corner of Teilo Street. This was demolished in 1898. It appeared on the Tithe Map of 1841, almost opposite one of the two inns in Canton at that time. The cottages faced the stepping stones that constituted the 'Pont' of 'Canna'.

The photograph above shows a flock of geese wandering past the rear of Canton Square in the 1890s. That below shows the frontage of the left of the square, which consisted of two sides of the tenements shown, with the rear of the manor house forming the third side, leaving the fourth side open to what is now Atlas Road. This was Canton's first 'modern' development, probably initiated by John Homfray who was the landowner. It was indeed called 'Homfray Square' in the census of 1851, when one occupant was John Kyte, an early policeman. The home of several members of long-standing Canton families, it was demolished before the end of the nineteenth century.

Cardiff in 1801 had been little more than a village with less than 2,000 people, many of whom would doubtless have agreed with Iolo Morganwg's description of it as 'that obscure and inconsiderable town'. But already the opening of the Glamorganshire Canal in 1794 had solved the problem of the Cardiff customs officer who had declared twelve years earlier: 'we have no coal exports, nor ever shall, as it would be too expensive to bring it down from the internal part of the country'. The construction of the canal gave 'a most notable impulse to Cardiff, bringing with it a wave of enthusiasm and of business' which led in the decade before 1800 to the town receiving a racecourse, a new bridge over the Taff, and its first printing press, bank and daily mail-coach to London. The canal had been constructed by the iron-masters and iron was the first important export from Cardiff. The fortune and fame of the town would, however, be made by coal – a commodity whose value to the nation was recognised by the enormous block of it weighing 24 tons which in 1851 was displayed in the entrance hall to the Crystal Palace next to a statue of King Richard 'the Lionheart'. Coal and iron were the two prime materials of the Industrial Revolution, and the valleys of South Wales provided them both in abundance. Cardiff was a natural outlet for the valleys, and its exports soared as the revolution gathered pace and spread across the world. The potential was spotted by John Crichton Stuart, the 2nd Marquess of Bute (and his surveyor David Stewart) who risked his entire personal fortune to build the first of the Cardiff docks, opened in 1839. The role of the Butes in the growth of Cardiff is virtually unique. In the words of John Davies, extracted from his Cardiff and the Marquesses of Bute: 'Their activity here places them in the front rank of British city makers, for of the British cities in whose development a single landowning family played a preponderant role, Cardiff is undoubtedly the largest'. The gamble of the Marquess succeeded, and when coal took over from iron as the major export from Cardiff – following the relentless call for the 'black diamond' – the family's fortune and the town's success were assured. There were, of course, those who were unable to share in the rising prosperity of the town, and often for them the workhouse was the last resort. The workhouse was typical of both the architecture and the philosophy of the Victorians. It was designed to discourage entrants by deliberately offering them a standard of living below the least they could expect to find from the most menial employment outside. They were thus encouraged to find work and help themselves; 'self-help' and laissez-faire being two cornerstones of the Victorian creed. Many workhouse masters took things too far and the institutions inspired such dread that often men chose gaol as a preferable alternative. The workhouse at Canton, shown here around 1899, was built in 1839 to serve a union of 44 parishes reaching from the Vale up to Radyr and eastwards to St Mellons.

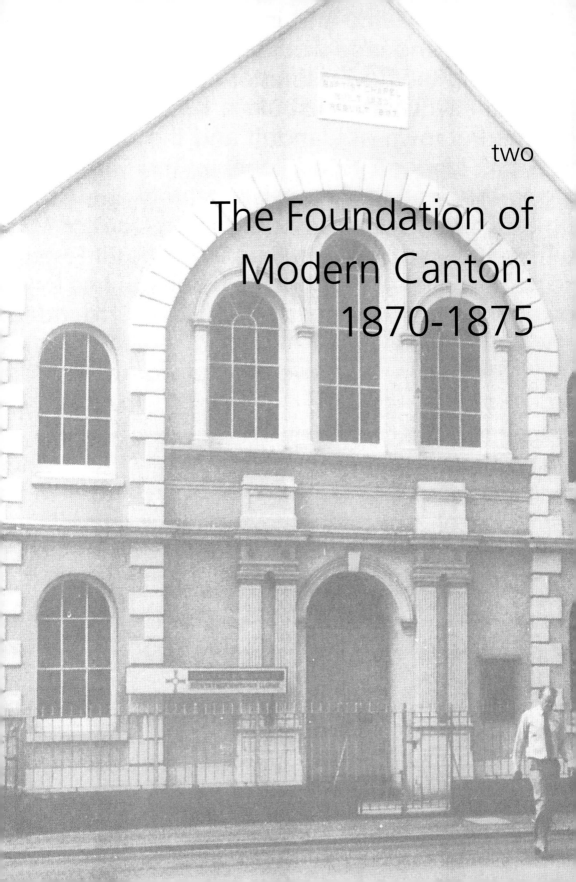

two

The Foundation of Modern Canton: 1870-1875

This period probably represented Victorian Britain at its most buoyant, with an optimism well expressed by the Great Exhibition of 1851 for which six million tickets were sold. The birth of the Industrial Revolution here had enabled Britain to become the richest and most powerful nation on earth, a process which was now reaching its peak. It was a notable time in Cardiff, and in Canton, too. The opening of the Bute West Dock in 1839, followed two years later by the Taff Vale Railway, enabled trade to expand rapidly as coal began to replace iron as the foremost export. The South Wales Railway reached Cardiff in 1850, linking it with London and leading later to the development of one of the two largest employers in Canton. Local communications were facilitated by the widening of Cardiff Bridge in 1859 and the provision by the Borough of horse buses in 1872 thereby offering the first cheap public transport (privately-operated horse buses had been running since 1855). It was, of course, from the docks that the success of Cardiff emanated, and these received a fresh impetus with the increasingly extensive exploitation of steam coal from the Cynon and Rhondda valleys after the 1850s. This was smokeless steam coal of the best quality which would soon be given the Admiralty's seal of approval in preference to its rival from Newcastle. Bute opened a second dock in 1858 and exports of coal rose from under a million tons in 1851 to over five million in 1881; Cardiff was by then well on its way to becoming the greatest coal port in the world. Men and their families in their thousands flocked here to share in the work and wealth created by the docks and between 1851 and 1861 the population of the town doubled from 20,000 to 40,000 and was to double twice more by 1901; in fact, in the century from 1801 the population multiplied one-hundred-fold. Overcrowding, however, caused some of the worst slums in Britain, and the town necessarily began to spill over and swallow up some of the surrounding hamlets. Canton, on the west bank of the Taff, was one of them and from 1850 it began to grow apace with the town a mile down the road.

It was in this period 1850-1875 that the foundation of modern Canton was laid, illustrated well by Waring's Map of 1869 which shows 29 streets alongside the two roads and three lanes of twenty years before. The distinctive character of the area was being moulded from the onset, when it was chosen by the National Land Freehold Society for their first venture in Wales. The policy of the three major land-owning families in Cardiff (Bute, Windsor Clive and Tredegar) was to adopt 99-year leases, which were therefore unusually predominant in the town. The aim of the National Land Freehold Society, however, was to provide small freeholds and so increase the numbers of those holding the franchise, and in pursuit of this it purchased 110 acres of land for £14,100 at the sale of the Romilly Estate in 1852. The estate was auctioned partly as farmland, but in Canton as 'good sites for building' particularly as 'country villas for merchants'. This purchase meant that the area around Conway Road and Severn Grove contained the only freehold land in Cardiff, a fact reflected in the variety of the nature of its houses and their architecture, which contrasts with the much more uniform impression presented by the development on Bute and other land in Canton and elsewhere in Cardiff.

However, the picture was not one of progress unalloyed: Sam Allen, in his Reminiscences, recalled that when he first knew Canton in 1860 'it consisted of very few streets, such as Severn Road, the houses of which had only just been built and were for the most part untenanted and in a great state of dilapidation, many of them quite uninhabitable'. But this was not typical, and the population which had been 250 in 1841 rose to 1,000 in 1851 and then to 10,000 in 1871. It was already assuming the nature ascribed to it in the 1880s which seems to have been true of it ever since – that of 'a broad social mix mainly notable for its respectable artisan and lower-middle-class character'.

The Founders of Ferndale.

David Davis of Maesyffynon. David Davis of Blaengwawr. Lewis Davis of Ferndale.

Of the eighteen or so 'large houses' of Canton, 'Preswylfa' ('dwelling') in Clive Road is the largest and has the most significant story (see p. 41). The house was built around 1867 by Lewis Davis, who became head of the great coal-owning company of David Davis & Sons, a household name in South Wales during the last quarter of the nineteenth century – but not to be confused with that of that other great Welsh magnate, David Davies of Llandinam. The company had been founded by David Davis, with Lewis and his brother (also David) as partners. This was after the father had been one of the first to strike the famous four-foot seam in the Rhondda which then remained, particularly in its upper reaches, a place of farms and fields. The company acquired a reputation not only as a prosperous commercial enterprise but also as one that cared for its employees: 'Lewis and David took a friendly and sympathetic interest in all that affected their workmen; shared in all their joys and sorrows and helped them with wise and loving counsel; participating in every movement which tended to promote the health, education, progress and highest prosperity of the community'. Lewis Davis lived at 'Preswylfa' for four years, during which his thanksoffering of £1,000 to the Wesley Cardiff Circuit led to Conway Road Methodist Church being built, as £700 of his gift was earmarked for that purpose.

Llandaff Road Baptist Church was the first place of worship built in Canton. That two of the first three were Welsh-speaking reinforces the impression that the Welsh language was a more powerful element in the community than is usually realised, and the fact that 73 per cent of the field names on the Tithe Map were in the Welsh tongue suggests that this was even more true of the earlier hamlet. The chapel in Llandaff Road was opened on 26 December 1853 as an offshoot of the Tabernacl Welsh Baptist Church in the Hayes – whose Canton members had previously met in a thatched cottage nearby. The building was renovated in the 1890s prior to the Pastorate being undertaken by Revd Robert Lloyd ('Lloyd Casbach'), hailed as an 'Apollo' of the Welsh pulpit and President of the Welsh Baptist Union in 1884. He converted into English the services which had hitherto been held in Welsh, and set the church on a sound footing before he retired in 1918. 'J.C.' Evans was the best-known and longest-serving (1938-58) of the later pastors, who also included Revd J. Elfed Davies and Revd Julie Hopkins – the first woman minister in Canton. In 1995 the church united with New Trinity United Reform Church to form the Canton Uniting Church, and the building in Llandaff Road is now occupied by the Cardiff Chinese Christian Church. The novelist Howard Spring's first description of home is that of a cottage in Chapel Court beside the chapel (preface to the second edition of Heaven Lies About Us).

The Llandaff School for the Deaf and the Dumb occupied the two houses in Romilly Crescent, on the corner of Llandaff Road, from 1866 until 1906. It was one of only two such institutions in Wales and twelve throughout Britain. In its forty years it enabled almost a hundred pupils to live comparatively fulfilled and happy lives. Well-supported by both humble and high in the local community, it was run by Alexander Melville and his wife and, in the words of the Western Mail, it 'reflected honour upon Cardiff'.

Some of William Symonds' workmen building the Canton Market extension fronting Carmarthen Street, at the turn of the century. The first Whitsun Fair at Canton Market at its opening, in 1859, drew 500 cattle, as many sheep, and 600 horses. It was celebrated with a band sent by Wyndham Lewis and a display of pyrotechnics by Professor Burns of the Bristol Zoological Gardens, which ended with the grand set piece May Canton Prosper.

Sir William Goscombe John was born on 2 February 1860 at No 3 Union Street – which later became Gray Street. His father, Thomas, was a woodcarver in the workshops set up by the 3rd Marquess of Bute to restore Cardiff Castle, and William followed in his footsteps there. He continued his studies at London and first found success with the Gold Medal and Travelling Scholarship of the Royal Academy in 1889. This enabled him to take a studio in Paris, where he watched Rodin at work. His work was that of a fine craftsman and an academic sculptor whose art was a compound of realism and romanticism. It won him many honours both at home and abroad and included commissions for numerous public statues, and for the Salisbury tomb in Westminster Abbey. He also designed the regalia for the Investiture of the Prince of Wales in 1911, and the Great Seal of King Edward VIII in 1936. In 1909 he was elected an Academician of the Royal Academy. He was knighted in 1911 for his services to Welsh culture and in 1936, in company with the Earl of Plymouth, he received the Freedom of the City of Cardiff for his services to the city and to Wales. Sir William died in London on 15 December 1952. He sculpted Joyance – the figure of the boy – in Thompson's Park and there are many of his works in Cardiff, including his representation of St David, which is said to be the most successful of the group of eleven figures commissioned by Lord Rhondda in the City Hall. The illustration is of his self-portrait and includes on the base a sketch of his sculpture The Elf – 'his idealised view of the Edwardian Woman'.

Revd Vincent Saulez, of Huguenot descent, who entered the ministry after holding an army commission in India. He became the first Rector of Canton (St John the Evangelist) in 1863 and not only built up his own church but was instrumental in founding St Paul's (Grangetown) and St Catherine's churches. The affection and respect he inspired for putting the care of his people first was reflected in the crowds who attended his funeral in 1889, overflowing from the church and gathering in the surrounding crescent, whilst large numbers lined the route of the procession to the Llandaff Cathedral. It seems likely that Ethel and Daisy streets were named after his daughters in honour of his efforts to provide decent, inexpensive housing for the Irish population at a time when the slums of the town were being cleared.

The Canton National School, operated under the auspices of the Church of England, was the first school in Canton, and opened in 1856 on the site of the present Parish Hall in Leckwith Road. It nurtured three knights – Sir William Goscombe John, Sir John Ballinger (librarian), and Sir Charles Melhuish (Lord Mayor of Cardiff in 1931) – and was known affectionately as 'The Leckwith College' of the 1860s. Before the Cathedral School was opened in 1880 it provided the choristers of Llandaff Cathedral. The building was demolished in 1962 not long after it had ceased to function as a school.

Canton's parish church of St John the Evangelist arose at the inspiration of Bishop Alfred Ollivant of Llandaff; it was designed by Pritchard & Seddon, the architects responsible for the restoration of the cathedral – which had hitherto served as the parish church of Canton. Of a style typical of the Victorian Gothic revival, with a graceful spire, John Hilling claims it is the most completely successful of John Pritchard's Cardiff churches. The nave was consecrated on 6 March 1855 but the building as a whole was not completed until 1871.

Pendyris House in Conway Road (see below) was named by Louis Tylor (who lived there from 1883 to 1887) of the family from whom Tylorstown took its name; Tylorstown colliery was at Pendyrus in the Rhondda Fach. He came to Cardiff from London in 1876 to take charge of the collieries owned by the firm of Tylor & Lewis of which he was a partner. Once here, he became President of the Cardiff Naturalists' Society and the second Treasurer of University College, Cardiff. He was also an early exponent of a scheme to provide an old age allowance for the miners of South Wales.

Pendyris House, No 56 Conway Road, was occupied after Louis Tylor by Henry Lynch Blosse, who remained there until Dr James Mullin took up residence in 1895 (see p. 45). The house remained in the doctor's family until 1981, when it was demolished to make way for a sheltered housing development which opened in 1982. The coach house of 'Pendyris' was converted to a motor repair garage, which became a road transport firm's warehouse in the 1930s and ended its life as an HGV driving school.

Solomon Andrews began in business selling sweets from trays but soon rose and diversified. He entered the field of transport in 1863, and was running, building and exporting buses before long. This photograph of 1900 shows one of his horse buses in Canton on its way from Cardiff Castle to The Black Lion in Llandaff; the route followed Wyndham Crescent, Severn Grove, Mortimer Road, Conway Road and Penhill, where an extra 'cock' horse was used to assist the ascent. This horse-bus service ran half-hourly, could carry 26 passengers and continued until the First World War.

The first three schools in Canton were provided by the churches, and that of St Mary's, which opened on 13 June 1869, was the second. It also served as a 'mass centre' before the 'old church' was built on the same site around 1874. The foundation stone of the new school was laid on 7 October 1928. The photograph shows an attentive class in the first few years of the twentieth century.

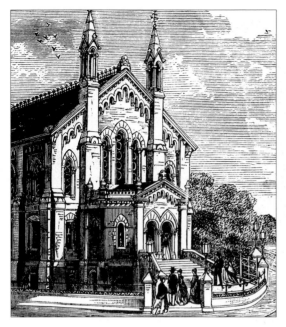

The architect's impression of Conway Road Methodist Church, which opened on 1 December 1869. This fine building was referred to as 'one of the Cathedrals of Methodism' by Dr Maldwyn Edwards when he was chairman of the district. A member of another chapel nearby expressed a similar thought when he said that Capel Salem in Market Road felt like a cathedral of the denomination, and it has often been said that the parish church of St John's has the air of a cathedral – which all suggests that Canton is well endowed with ecclesiastical dignity.

What is now the Gospel Hall on the corner of Llandaff Road and Romilly Road was opened on 19 July 1859 by the Methodist congregation in Canton as their temporary home while the church in Conway Road was being built. It was intended to convert the hall into housing afterwards. However, after the Methodists moved out in 1869, it was rented by the minister and a group of members from the Welsh Congregational Chapel in Severn Road who felt that the needs of the neighbourhood would best be served with services in English – and hence parted from those who did not agree. In 1894 this group amalgamated with the Trinity Church from the town centre to form New Trinity Church in Cowbridge Road, Canton. The hall was then taken over by the Plymouth Brethren who have been there ever since. Howard Spring recalls that the Brethren used to pray for 'those Wesleyans who attend Conway Road in their top hats'.

The Founders of the Cause

Mr. JAMES HERNE
1859-1907
Treasurer of Chapel Building Fund,
Class Leader and Trustee, Sunday
School Superintendent.

Mrs. JAMES HERNE
1859-
Daughter of Mr. B. Wright
now in her 90th year

Mr. BENJAMIN WRIGHT
1859-1882   Class Leader and Trustee

(The dates mentioned throughout this Booklet, unless otherwise stated, give the period of connection with the Church.)

In 1858 a committee of Charles Street Chapel was appointed to obtain a preaching place in Canton, and within a year a chapel on the corner of Llandaff Road and Romilly Road was provided by Benjamin Wright of St Nicholas (the father of Mrs James Herne). James Herne of Suffolk House became the first Sunday school superintendent and Mr Wright moved to a cottage in the grounds of Suffolk House and became a class leader and trustee. Mr Lewis Davis of 'Preswylfa' gave £700 in 1867 towards the construction of a new and larger church and in the same year Alderman William Sanders was appointed Secretary of the Building Fund Committee. The foundation stone of the church in Conway Road was laid on 31 March 1869 by Benjamin Wright – the great, great grandfather of Mrs Betty King who is now a leader in the church and who has in her keeping the engraved silver trowel with which the stone was laid. Within nine months the building was open for worship. It prospered with the help of prominent laymen such as W.E. Vaughan and F.J. Beavan; membership increased from 74 in 1869 to 450 in 1918 and 'daughter churches' were founded in Llandaff, Victoria Park, Clare Gardens and Ely. It was probably the most thriving of Canton's churches, at a time when the faith was flourishing throughout the land. Church attendance in Britain reached its historic height in the Victorian Age around 1880 (although in Wales this may have been later, c. 1907). The historian Sir Robert Ensor has said that: 'No-one will understand Victorian England who does not appreciate that it was one of the most religious of all civilised countries, with a Christianity that emphasised conduct: English merchants' reputation as the most honest in the world was earned because heaven and hell seemed as certain to them as tomorrow's sunrise, and the Last Judgement was as real as this week's balance sheet ... evangelism made other-worldliness an everyday conviction and pleasure took second place to duty'.

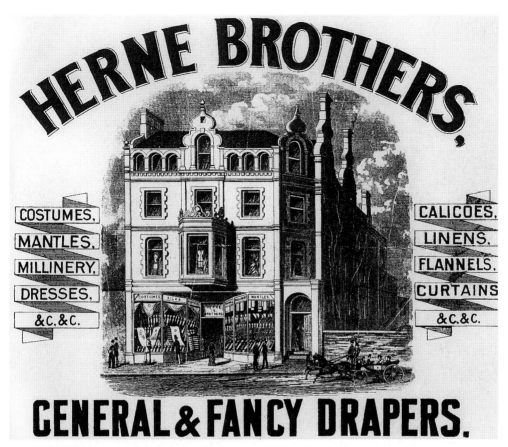

HERNE BROTHERS,

COSTUMES,
MANTLES,
MILLINERY,
DRESSES,
&C.&C.

CALICOES,
LINENS,
FLANNELS,
CURTAINS
&C.&C.

GENERAL & FANCY DRAPERS.

Above: Suffolk House, on the corner of Romilly Road and Llandaff Road, was built by Benjamin Wright as a wedding gift to his daughter and her husband James Herne. This is an advertisement from the 1880s for the Herne's drapery business in Queen Street, Cardiff.

Left: William Sanders, a Cardiff alderman and magistrate, came to Cardiff in 1854 from Doncaster as a Wesleyan teacher. However, in 1860 he started business as a pitwood agent and two years later became Secretary of the Principality Building Society - 'he was the Principality'. A prominent Liberal and a councillor for Canton, he became Mayor in 1889-90 and as such presided at the presen-tation of the Freedom of Cardiff to the Duke of Clarence when the Clarence Bridge was opened in Grangetown. He lived at Doncaster Villa, No 2 Conway Road (see p. 30).

An offshoot of Capel Seion (the first Calvinistic Methodist Chapel in Cardiff) which stood on the site of the Old Library, Capel Salem was the third place of worship built in Canton and is now the only one remaining where Welsh is the language of its services. Its foundation stone in Albert Street was laid on 16 July 1856, on land partly given by Edward Priest Richards whose name provided the earlier one for the street. The chapel was built by John Davies, a member, to a simple design inspired by the Tabernacl in the Wilderness, and the traditional Plygain ('Dawn') service there was held on Christmas morning, 1856. Its first deacon was Morgan Lewis, who came from Bristol to take responsibility for the House of Refuge, and John Evans (father-in-law of Jacob Davies) was the first Secretary. In 1860, Revd Edward Mathews, Ewenni, came to live in Canton and he took a great interest in the cause, improving the structure of the chapel to bring it a new dignity. Membership grew after receiving an impetus from the revival of 1859. It was, however, reduced at the turn of the century when a small group of members transferred to the chapel in Cathedral Road because the services there were held in English. Nevertheless, in 1908 Salem could still claim 165 members with 157 pupils in its Sunday school. At that time the Calvinistic Methodists were building many new chapels in Cardiff, and the people of Salem felt ready to think about a larger premises for themselves. With the help of Charles Radcliffe they acquired a plot of ground in Cowbridge Road which had been used in the 1860s for 'The Prophets' School' of Revd Edward Mathews. This had later become the workshop and yard of two chapel members. The pattern of growth in Cardiff at this time was to build a schoolroom first and, if it was successful, to erect a chapel afterwards. The school was opened in May 1910 and the chapel followed quickly. Its architect was Edgar Fawckner of the Newport firm of Habershon & Fawckner, and the builder was James Stephens, who had earlier been given the task of re-siting the castle wall adorned by the animals. Capel Salem was his masterpiece, constructed with grey stone from Pontnewydd quarry complemented with Bath stone corners and window eves. In contrast to the simplicity of the first chapel, the new one imparted a sense of being a 'cathedral of the denomination', which was remarked upon by Revd J.A. Evans of Cardiff and many others. A high tower was erected to adorn the building. At its foot is the foundation stone laid by Mr Henry Radcliffe, JP, of 'Druidhouse', on 21 May 1910. Salem is well known as the chapel of the 'Novello' family, where all its members took a full part and Madame Clara played the organ. She was the grand-daughter of an archetypal silver-tongued Welsh preacher, Revd William Evans of Tonyrefail, who refused to baptise his grandchild with the 'heathen' name of Clara Novello – chosen by her father, Jacob Davies, in tribute to the famous Italian soprano who he had heard and enjoyed in Cardiff. It was in Salem that Ivor Novello's parents were married on 31 October 1883, and there that he was baptised. The photograph shows the first chapel in Albert Street, on the corner of Philip Street, at the turn of the century. Behind it is the National School.

This is the architect's impression of the original Hope Baptist Chapel in Cowbridge Road (now Calvary), which was an offshoot of Bethany, the first Baptist church in Cardiff. Its members first met in 1858 and the first pastor was appointed in 1860. The chapel was raised in the early 1860s at a cost of £1,100, of which £600 was contributed by the Bethany congregation. The pastor at the turn of the century, Revd T.W. Medhurst, was C.H. Spurgeon's first pupil, and a close friend. His son, Revd C. Spurgeon Medhurst, became a missionary in China.

The "distinctive" building in the centre of this photograph of Wellington Street in the 1960s began its life in the early 1870s as one of the British schools provided by the Nonconformist churches. Their appearance prompted the Church of England to respond with their National schools. It was the third of Canton's schools but was soon made redundant by the advent of state education and was taken over by the Salvation Army as their first 'Citadel' in Canton around 1882. It then became the John Cory Workmen's Institute, opened by Sir Clifford Cory in 1909, and finally served for decades as the Canton YMCA.

The lodge at the southern entrance of Sophia Gardens. It was built in 1857 but destroyed by an air raid in 1941 and replaced by the red-brick bungalow that now stands nearby. The second lodge in Sophia Close has been used for various purposes and is now a restaurant.

View from the clock tower of Cardiff Castle, looking westwards over Canton, *c.*1871. Leckwith Hill provides the background to the left, leading on to the ridge which extends to Caerau. Sheep graze on the east bank of the Taff towards the foreground, and a solitary cow ambles beside the river near the centre of the photograph. It provides an illustration of the stage of development of Canton at that time, and enlarged sections of it are shown on the next two pages.

Cathedral Road had not been developed when this photograph was taken, and its most notable feature then would have been Plasturton farmhouse, which was demolished in 1895. It was referred to as the 'capital messuage' (chief household) of an inferior manor reaching back at least to the sixteenth century. Three points of reference are the turret of the lodge destroyed by bombs in 1941, far left centre of picture; the fountain in Sophia Gardens far right centre; and Conway Road Chapel and its two spirelets top right corner.

Some of the interest in this photograph lies in the absence of development at Riverside. Only the partially completed houses of Mark Street, Wyndham Street and Lewis Street encroach upon its fields, whilst Leckwith Road marks the limit of the background housing.

The spire of St John the Evangelist is a landmark, top centre, and a little below it the Wyndham Hotel stands tall and clear at the junction of Wellington Street and Cowbridge Road. The junction of Cathedral Road and Cowbridge Road just appears on the right, near to where David Lewis was keeping the tollgate in 1865. The latter road curves towards Cardiff (Canton) Bridge, showing Westbourne Crescent on the left and the remains of the old bridge to the right.

This photograph of Cardiff Bridge in 1891 shows the remains of the 1796 bridge. The first stone bridge – to replace the earlier wooden structures often destroyed by debris brought down by floods – was probably raised in 1582 and rebuilt after damage caused in the Civil War. A new bridge built in 1796 was destroyed by floods about 1827, causing traffic to be diverted through Llandaff. A new and wider bridge was built in 1859, and widened twice afterwards – in 1877 and 1931. Although commonly called Canton Bridge, it is more correctly known as Cardiff (Canton) Bridge.

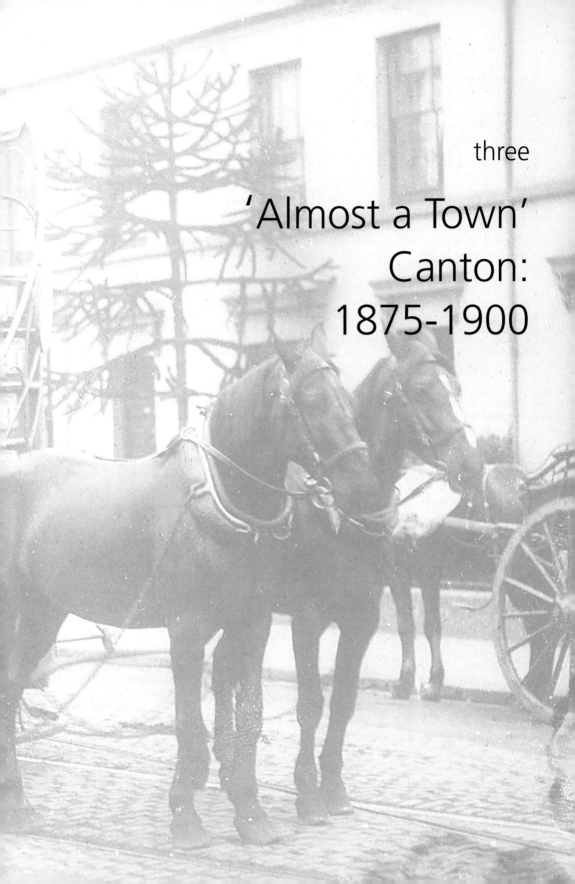

three

'Almost a Town'
Canton:
1875-1900

The optimism of the previous quarter-century was now tempered by periods of trade depression and the dawning realisation that Britain's lucrative monopoly of the Industrial Revolution could not last indefinitely. Towards the end of the period the confidence of the country was shaken by the South African (Boer) War. After the exhilaration and uncertainties of becoming the world's first industrial and urban nation, Britons could now take a calmer look around them, and what they saw was not always pleasant. Charles Booth caused a shock in 1899 when he revealed that almost one in three of the people in London - the world's richest city - were living below the poverty line. Private initiative such as that shown by Dr T.J. Barnardo and the Salvation Army was a typical Victorian response. The government did, however, address some of the greatest needs with the Public Health Act of 1875 and W.E. Forster's Elementary Education Act of 1870 which made provision for the first time for the education of all children. Government action was also beginning to be influenced by the granting for the first time of the vote to working-class householders in towns in 1867, and to those in the country in 1884. Behind all this, however, an overall sense of well-being still held sway. It was expressed in the celebrations of Victoria's golden and diamond jubilees, when there was a recognition that the Queen stood for much that was great in Britain. Commentators searched as far back as King Alfred to find a comparable monarch.

The first Act of Parliament concerned exclusively with Wales was the Welsh Sunday Closing Act of 1881. It caused a real furore at Cardiff, in which the Thompson family played a leading role. Charles Thompson was typical of the businessmen drawn to Cardiff by the trade created by the docks, where exports of coal continued to rise -
from over 5 million tons in 1881 to over 7 million in 1901. The population of the town continued to rise too, and the largest increase in numbers - from 82,761 in 1881 to 128,915 in 1891 - occurred at this time. The Corporation took in hand the 'virtual' towns that had sprung up around it with the Cardiff Improvement Act of 1875. The increasing status of the Borough was recognised when it became a County Borough in 1888; the singular importance of coal in its development was illustrated by the opening of the coal exchange in Mount Stuart Square in 1886; and the Dowlais Works, the only major industry in Cardiff, was opened five years later. The cultural life of the town flourished also, as the Free Library, Museum and Art Gallery and School of Science and Art was opened in 1882 in what is now the Old Library, and a year later Cardiff was chosen in preference to Swansea as the site of the University College of South Wales and Monmouthshire. Meanwhile, the restoration of the Castle had been completed by the romantic medievalist William Burges for the 3rd Marquess of Bute (a scholar well able to indulge his taste for art and architecture as he was possibly the richest man in Britain). The restoration was accompanied by the protection of farm land immediately north of the Castle, which helped secure for Cardiff the green heart which survives today.

The green, open spaces of Canton were, however, disappearing rapidly at this period of its greatest growth. The population more than doubled from 14,797 in 1881 to 32,805 in 1891, and 82 new streets appeared during this decade - 18 in the year 1885 alone. By the turn of the century, most of the Canton that we see around us today had come into being. The hamlet was incorporated into the Borough in 1875 and soon was to be described as almost a town in itself. This was not far-fetched considering what had come into the area by this time: near the centre was Canton Market, which was taken over by Cardiff Corporation in 1875 and acquired a slaughterhouse, close to the fortress-like police station (1883) and the County Police headquarters (1871). The railway depot became (with the Paper Mill, 1865) the joint largest employer in Canton, and there was a horse-tram depot in Cathedral Road. The first (temporary) library opened in Llandaff Road in 1891, soon after the first of the Board schools had appeared. When Cardiff became the first borough in Wales to provide a public electricity supply in 1885, the generating station was built in Eldon Road (which became Ninian Park Road).

Above left: Clara Novello Davies was born on 7 April 1861, the daughter of Jacob Davies, founder of the Blue Ribbon Choir. She began her musical career as a pianoforte accompanist and, because of her talent, was appointed to accompany the Cardiff United Choir of her father, and his Blue Ribbon Choir – so named because of its success at competitions in the Crystal Palace. She also taught the piano and singing to pupils who went on to great successes at eisteddfodau. She formed a ladies choir in 1893 which, in the same year, won a prize at the Chicago World Fair. The choir was allowed to use the prefix 'Royal' the following year after delighting the Queen at a command performance. Soon afterwards the *Manchester Guardian* said that 'it may fairly be regarded as one of the most striking features of musical Britain'. Madame Clara was known widely as 'Pencerddes Morganwg' ('Chief Musician of Glamorgan'), her name in the Gorsedd of Bards. After their marriage, she and her husband David moved to their house in Cowbridge Road – 'Llwyn yr Eos' or 'the Grove of Nightingales.'

Above right: One of the most colourful characters in Cardiff dockland at its prime was Antonio Leonardo Trifone, the Count de Lucovich. A knight of the Order of Francis Joseph I and Admiral of the Noble Corps of the Bocchesi Mariners (instituted over a thousand years ago), Antonio de Lucovich was born at Cattario in Dalmazia, which was then part of the Austro-Hungarian Empire. It was intended he should follow his family into the legal profession. However, he disappointed them at the last moment by choosing a career in commerce and hence settled in Cardiff in 1850. Here he ran a business exporting coal to his native Adriatic until he died in 1913. He lived for many years in Penhill House, Llandaff Road.

Continued from previous page:

  Cowbridge Road was developing into a shopping centre; in 1875 the stretch between Lower Cathedral Road and Wellington Street had been occupied by a farm. Recreation was provided in Thompson's Park and Victoria Park (opened in 1891 and 1897 respectively), while the Corporation Hotel of 1889 would have passed muster as an 'hotel de ville' across the English Channel. From the vitality of this new community sprang the Canton Rugby Club (in the 1880s) and the Canton (later Cardiff) Male Choir (1897). Both are still thriving today.

David Ivor Davies was born at 'Llwyn yr Eos', Cowbridge Road, on Sunday 15 January 1893; in 1927 he changed his name by deed poll to Ivor Novello. The family later moved to their own newly-built house at No 11 Cathedral Road, to which they gave the same name. It is likely that Ivor's first music teacher there (other than his mother) was Alice Saulez, the widow of the first Rector of Canton, who lived a few doors away with her daughter and ran a small academy.

'Preswylfa', Clive Road, *c.*1890, with, outside H. Woolcott and Marion Thompson. Joel Spiller founded his flour business at Bridgewater in 1838 and opened his first flour mill at Cardiff in partnership with Samuel Browne in 1854, the year of the Crimean War. Boosted by the demands of war, the business flourished and Charles Thompson (1815-1889) of Bridgewater, joined the company in 1858. After the death of Spiller and the retirement of Browne, Thompson and his sons effectively became Spillers & Company, which grew to be one of the largest millers in the land and the originator of the 'Turog' loaf. In 1870 Charles Thompson Snr moved into 'the impressive house Preswylfa in the country between Cardiff and Llandaff', where his family of seven sons and one daughter grew up. His son, H. Woolcott Thompson (1848-1919) became a director of the company and its largest shareholder and continued to live in 'Preswylfa' after his parents died – as did his daughter Marion who had looked after them and did not marry. She became one of the foremost helpers of the School for the Deaf and Dumb in Romilly Crescent. Herbert (1856-1939) lived at Whitley Batch, overlooking Llandaff Fields. He wrote a history of Cardiff and became an alderman of the city and Treasurer and Vice-President of University College, Cardiff. James Pyke (1846-1897) became chairman of Spillers and a director of the Taff Vale Railway; an art connoisseur, collector and proselytist, he was the creator of the Turner House gallery in Penarth. The most widely known of the brothers, James Pyke's posthumous effect upon Canton was considerable; money from his bequest was used to purchase land at Llandaff Road as a sports' ground for the University College, and to purchase Dulwich House as a convalescent home for 'Tired Mothers and Sick Children', while his brother presented 6,000 books to the branch library at Canton in his memory. Charles Thompson Jnr (1851-1939) built and lived in Penhill Close. It was he who gave Thompson's Park (formerly his private garden) to the people of Cardiff and who, together with Herbert, contributed £5,000 towards purchasing Llandaff Fields for the public. When he died, Thompson family control of Spillers came to an end. When Turner House was presented to the National Museum of Wales, the Earl of Plymouth said: 'the members of the Thompson family have done more in the way of generous benefaction than probably any other family in South Wales'.

Halket Street in the 1890s. This street between Severn Road and Wyndham Crescent was later renamed Avon Street, and was finally demolished to make way for a car park. By the 1890s it had deteriorated badly, as this photographs shows. However, the housing was afterwards made good and the street appears in the photograph of VE Day celebrations on page 107.

There were some patches of poor conditions in Canton, but nothing to equal the plight that Irish immigrants had been subjected to in Cardiff during the middle of the nineteenth century. The Superintendent of Police testified that one lodging house held 54 people in four small rooms. Slum clearance did not begin until the 1880s, when many Irish families moved to Canton and became well established here. The visitor wearing a cassock in the photograph is probably one of Dean Vaughan's 'Doves' (see p. 58).

In 1875 Canton and Roath were incorporated into the Borough of Cardiff and, for the first time, the town became the largest in Wales. Canton and Cardiff share many things including having rivers as their boundaries. Historically, Canton was bounded by water on three sides as it once reached down to the Severn estuary. Something more salubrious than river water would have been served in the 'loving-cups', which were large drinking vessels passed round at banquets; sharing a common cup was a sign of friendship or 'loving'. The importance of the local rivers is represented on this fine loving cup presented to Cardiff by the 3rd Marquess of Bute in 1891. The base of the cup contains figures of the gods of the rivers Taff, Ely and Rhymney, while Sabrina, the goddess of the River Severn, is at the feet of 'Dame Cardiff' atop the cup.

The first public transport provided by the Borough came in the form of horse-buses in 1872, and six years later the first horse-tram reached Canton. One of the latter is shown in this photograph taken in the 1890s, in which the conductor is Charles Paull, of No 123 Ninian Park Road. He soon graduated to become a driver and is shown as such in the photograph on page 78.

William Symonds was born at Longbredy, Dorset in 1848 and settled in Cardiff after spending two years in the United States. He began his building business in 1880, just as house construction was reaching its peak, and became a member of Cardiff Council between 1889 and 1892. He is responsible for the only name of a street in Canton known to reflect an association with its builder; in Purbeck Street he used stone from the Purbeck quarries of his native county. He built No 17 Romilly Road for himself but decided it was too large and never took up residence there; it was given the name Llanover Hall after being acquired by the Corporation as the Juvenile Employment Centre for Girls *c.*1938.

The twenty acres of Victoria Park were planned on what had been previously Llandaff Common, not Ely Common as is usually recorded. The park was opened on 16 June 1897 and was given its name to commemorate the Diamond Jubilee of Queen Victoria six days later. It held two summer houses, a bandstand and a drinking fountain with an ornamental canopy, all of which could be found there in the Edwardian period when this photograph was taken.

Dr James Mullin, MA, MD, MCh, DPH, JP, was born in poverty in Cookstown, Ireland, at the start of the Great Irish Famine in 1846. His father died when the child was young, leaving the widow to provide for her family. James left school at eleven and undertook menial work but used all the time he could to study, working so hard that he was bent, with greying hair, by the age of twenty. A scholarship was won to Queen's College, Galway, and in 1874 he gained his BA with honours in literature and metaphysics. After further mixed studies he turned to medicine and obtained his MD in 1880. Dr Mullin came to Cardiff in the 1880s and built up a large practice, chiefly among the Irish population where he was known as a 'shilling doctor'. He cultivated his interest in politics and visitors to his house in Conway Road included Keir Hardie and Philip Snowden. He also pursued his literary interests, composing the National Eisteddfod prize poem in 1899 and also the words of *The Celtic Race for Ever* to music written by Dr Joseph Parry. Dr Mullin lived at Pendyris House, Conway Road (see p. 28) until his death on 19 December 1919. His autobiography, *The Story of a Toiler's Life* was published in 1921. The photograph shows him, centre, with, on his right, his good friend, Dr Benjamin Broad, (the first Superintendent of the Sanatorium) after whom Broad Street is named. He would have appreciated the tribute in the *Cardiff Times* by 'Idris', dedicated to a 'Physician, Poet, Patriot', and ending:

> His writings all would flavoured be
> With pure and deep humanity.
> His winning smile, his cheery grip,
> Are things not easy to let slip.
> Long shall we keep his image clear,
> Long shall we hold his memory dear.
> A heart unspoilt (deny who can) -
> A Brother, and a Friend of Man.

For almost a hundred years John Norman's business kept pace with a changing world: 1875 – wheelwright; 1882 – timber merchant and wheelwright; 1891 – Canton Steam Wheel Works; 1901 –

CANTON TIMBER YARD & WHEEL WORKS
MARKET ROAD.

JOHN NORMAN,

TIMBER MERCHANT.

COACH BUILDER AND

WHEELWRIGHT

OAK, ASH, & ELM PLANKS, SPOKES, STOCKS & FELLOES
ALWAYS FOR SALE.

Scantlings cut to order on the shortest notice.
NEW AND SECOND HAND CARTS AND TRAPS ALWAYS IN STOCK.
REPAIRS AND PAINTING PROMPTLY ATTENDED TO.

Canton Carriage and Wheelworks; 1909 – Canton Carriage Motor and Wheelworks; 1942 – John Norman Motors Limited. The business continued for almost a further twenty years in Market Road.

A fancy dress party outside St Vincent's Church in Daisy Street, *c.*1900. Daisy, a daughter of the first Rector of Canton, rented a room for prayer, Bible reading and hymn singing, and paid for it out of her pin money. On the window she painted 'St Vincent's Mission' choosing the name in honour of her father. From this sprang the iron Mission Church, and from that St Luke's, which still has some furniture and a chalice from St Vincent's (closed 1933).

General Gordon was to Victorians the 'hero of heroes', and the country was grief-stricken when he was killed in 1885 at Khartoum, the capital of the Sudan. The capital was recaptured by the British in 1898, which was the year when Lance-Corporal Samuel Vickery was awarded the Victoria Cross for conspicuous bravery during operations in the Sudan. The citation mentioned 'rescuing a wounded comrade under heavy fire' and 'killing three of the enemy who attacked him when separated from his company.' He lived at No 33 Romilly Crescent for twenty years from 1936 onwards, and neighbours can recall a further example of his bravery when he rescued several people from a burning house nearby.

Richard White and his two strikers – one of whom was his son Ewart – in the 1890s. Their forge occupied an old farm building in Albert Street Lane. The photograph was provided by his grand-daughter, Mrs Irene Stuart, who still has the indenture of his five-year apprenticeship with Walter Poole of Monknash, which began on 23 July 1874. Her husband Reg is related to the old Canton family of Gedrych and also to the Mathews family of Llandaff.

Clare Gardens Methodist Church began in 1883 when W.J. Sanders and C.E. Abbot of Conway Road Methodist Church hired a small shop at Beauchamp Street in Riverside. A larger loft in Tudor Lane was rented in 1886 and continued growth led to the erection of a school-chapel in Machen Place in 1887. The present church there was opened in 1898, and is shown in this pre-Second World War photograph. The small spire was lost when the building was damaged in the Blitz. The church has recently been renovated and its members now undertake a wide range of activities in the community.

The eleven acres of Thompson's Park, in Romilly Road, were originally the gardens of Charles Thompson, who opened them to the public in 1891 and gave them to the Corporation in 1912. Howard Spring writes of 'the man who had given the park to the public exercising his right to ride his horse therein – a white horse, and on it this man, who was always hatless, with close-cropped snow-white hair and a hale, austere face that I know now to have been like Emerson'.

This Bush family portrait was taken by J. Long, of No 63, Crockherb Town, Cardiff in June, 1888. He also took, and signed, the photograph of 'Preswylfa' on page 41. James and Fanny Bush were the first occupants of 'Bryn Asaph', No 15 Romilly Road, in 1890 and members of the family lived there until early 1995. James Bush was born at Carmarthen where he attended the National school, first as a pupil and then as a pupil-teacher. After taking the art master's certificate he opened the first science and art classes at Newport in 1865 and was immediately asked by the Cardiff Free Library committee to begin classes here. These flourished and became the technical college of the town, with Mr Bush as headmaster of the art school. This led eventually to the University of Wales Institute of Science and Technology, and James Bush became one of the most influential people in the development of technical teaching in Cardiff. Fanny, who had also trained as an artist, was Secretary of the Glamorgan branch of the Welsh Industries Association. Three of their sons were students of the arts and science classes. Reginald (the eldest) and Frederick (in the foreground of the photograph) specialised in art: the former becoming the headmaster of the Bristol Municipal School of Art, and the latter the organising art master for the secondary schools of the West Riding of Yorkshire. Archibald, the youngest, specialised in technical work and became the chief engineer of Mombasa for the Public Works Department of the British East Africa Protectorate. He was as famous as a lion-hunter as he was an engineer. Percy, educated at University College, Cardiff, became very well known as a rugby player. He captained Cardiff in 1905-6 (Cardiff's 'Invincible Season') and first played for Wales against the New Zealand 'All Blacks' side in 1905. Emigrating to Nantes in 1910, he eventually became Deputy Consul at the British Consulate there, before returning to Cardiff in 1939. Ethel Maud, who inherited the house, was a graduate of the University of London, and taught English and religious studies at Howell's School, Llandaff. She is remembered there, amongst many other things, for taking a portable pulpit to Llandaff Fields at a time when it seemed to be the 'Speakers Corner' of South Wales.

Colonel Charles Harrison Page, JP, who was made a Knight of the Imperial Russian Order of Saint Stanislaus, in recognition of twenty-five years service as Russian Vice-Consul in Cardiff. He came here in 1852 and for forty years ran a coal exporting company. One of the founders of the Cardiff Chamber of Commerce in 1865, and vice-chairman of the Cardiff Workmen's Cottage Company, he served for twenty-three years in the 2nd Glamorgan Artillery Volunteers. He lived at Dulwich House, Pencisely Road.

Revd D. Tyssil Evans, MA, BSc, was born in Pembrokeshire, of a line of preachers, and came to Cardiff as Lecturer in Hebrew at University College. A vibrant personality full of humour and wisdom, he became closely involved with all New Trinity's members and activities as soon as he was appointed its first minister in 1894. A 'modernist' able to assimilate the new scientific and critical ideas of his time, he was yet able to preserve the simple faith of his flock in a sceptical period. Under his leadership the fellowship fairly hummed with activity and membership more than doubled in his first ten years – which witnessed 29 newcomers in the year of the 1905 religious revival. In 1912 he became Chairman of the South Wales English Congregational Union and published his *Principles of Hebrew Grammar* before ill-health forced his early retirement.

This silver communion cup, hallmarked 1677, was presented to Trinity Church by John Archer, a prosperous Cardiff businessman who was one of the aldermen nominated in the charter of King James II in 1687. It was Archer who leased the ground on which Trinity was built. He also gave it £400, in order that the interest should be used for a minister and to help the poor. The cup was transferred to Canton and then donated to the Welsh Folk Museum at St Fagans.

New Trinity is the successor to Cardiff's oldest Nonconformist church – Trinity Congregational Church – founded in 1640. Its first leaders risked their livelihoods and their lives for their faith and the freedom to follow it. Revd David Williams was its minister for 50 years when John and Charles Wesley were frequent visitors to Cardiff. An active supporter of the Revival, he built and lent the chapel at Watford near Caerphilly which played a significant role in the development of Welsh Calvinistic Methodism. Towards the end of the last century, Trinity members found that their site was becoming untenable. A group of English Congregationalists meeting in Canton had purchased a plot of ground on the corner of Theobald Road and the two parties united to found 'New Trinity' Congregational Church, which opened on 11 October 1894.

R.P. Culley was the caterer at a Plymouth army camp when he was asked by Sir Edward Hill, commanding the Glamorgan Artillery Volunteers: 'Why don't you come and start business in Cardiff?' He did, and opened the restaurant in the Coal Exchange. Then he opened a grocery and wine business, which included a store at No 96 Cowbridge Road. After that he bought the Great Western Hotel. At the Fine Art, Industrial and Maritime Exhibition of 1896 in Cathays Park, he not only provided the refreshments but also the entertainment – which included electric launches on a canal carrying visitors to an illuminated lake, where a costume opera with a cast of one hundred performed every night. In the 1890s Mr Culley lived at Lydford House, Cathedral Road.

Charles Gooch was the son of Sir Daniel Gooch, the engineer who opened the Swindon works with Isambard Kingdom Brunel and who became chairman of the Great Western Railway. Charles came to Cardiff in 1875 to take charge of the GWR collieries and became a magistrate in the town. Previously, he had worked in Russia with the New Russia Company's iron and steel works and collieries. This development was pioneered in 1869 by John Hughes of Merthyr in the Donetz Valley of the Ukraine. The town which sprang up there housed large numbers of workmen from South Wales, and was named Hughesovka (it later became Stalino). In the 1890s Charles Gooch lived at 'Campville', Cathedral Road.

Cathedral Road has become recognised as one of the finest Victorian highways in Britain and one of the most desirable of Cardiff addresses. But it was not always so: hitherto it had been Pontcanna Lane, with Plasturton Farm at the south end, Pontcanna Farm at the north end, and John Terrell, cowkeeper, living in between. Terrell's address was recorded as Cathedral Road even as late as 1871. The most concentrated development in the road took place between 1885 and 1900, when the number of houses rose from 16 to over 200. At first these were the homes of many of the wealthiest business families in Cardiff, such as Marment, Crouch, Lermon, Rapport, Cohen, Rivlin, Bradnum, Bowles, Robert Bevan and A.E. Harris. Other later residents well-known in Cardiff and beyond included the lawyer Sir Charles Hallinan, the architect Sir Percy Thomas and doctors Strachan, Byron Evans and Buist (the Police Surgeon).

The fine villas were soon acquired for other than domestic purposes, and this trend accelerated as the wealth of Cardiff declined and the houses became too expensive for families to purchase and maintain. Doctors' and other medical practices began to increase after the First World War and the road became the seat for many centres of national and local government departments (such as the Ministry of Information) and the Welsh headquarters of such bodies as the Church in Wales, the Automobile Association and the St John's Ambulance Brigade. Small private hotels were not common until the 1950s, although several private schools and hospitals had appeared before then. In the middle of this century, the road began to suffer from some inappropriate modern development, which was fortunately restrained by the efforts of the Victorian Society of Cardiff. The previous page shows two typical early residents of the road.

This photograph of Cowbridge Road in 1940 shows, on the left, part of the County Police headquarters for Glamorgan. It was built in 18 71 and served as the Police headquarters until 1946. It then became the Glamorgan Motor Tax Office until it was demolished in 1963. It was from here that Colonel L.A. Lindsay, the Chief Constable of Glamorgan, commanded police operations during the 'Great Unrest' immediately before the First World War. The memorial to those who died in that war can be seen top left.

Severn Road School, c.1903. This was the first of the state (Board) schools in Canton, and was opened in May 1882, enlarged in 1890 and again in 1899. Its pupils included many who would become well-known, including the journalist and novelist Howard Spring; the politician and novelist Maurice Edelman and the footballer Ernie Curtis.

Buffalo Bill crossing Cardiff Bridge into Canton at the turn of the century. Colonel William Cody came to Cardiff three times: in 1891, 1903 and 1904. Sharpshooter Annie Oakley accompanied him on his first two visits, when his show attracted audiences of up to 22,000. He also visited other nearby towns and said: 'No one can help admiring the beautiful choral singing that I have heard in Wales. I was very much struck with the "Sospan Fach" by the audience at Llanelly'. In Cardiff, his entourage of several hundred, accompanied by hundreds of horses, set up camp in Sophia Gardens.

The old Canton police station which was demolished in 1962, soon after this photograph was taken. It had been built in 1883 by the Dunn family of builders who lived almost directly opposite in Cowbridge Road, and was of stone, similar in appearance to the contemporary Corporation Hotel. In its prime, Canton was a 'Superintendent's Station' and the headquarters of 'B' division. Those were the days when 'everyone walked and the inspector rode his bike to inspect the troops'.

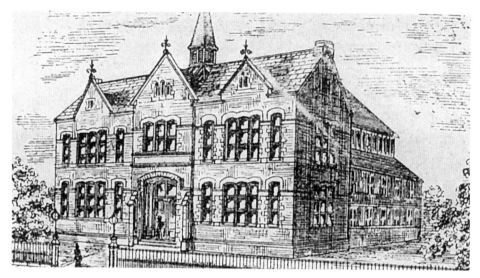

The 'Wesley Centenary School' in Conway Road opposite the Methodist church was opened in 1893, to accommodate 700 Sunday scholars and provide an assembly hall and lecture room. To provide for that number of pupils may seem incredible today, but in fact there were 746 scholars in 1899, with an average attendance of 453. Mr James Herne was followed as Sunday school superintendent by W.J. Sanders and Isaac Padfield. The building now houses 'Aelwyd Caerdydd', the Cardiff home of Urdd Gobaith Cymru (the Welsh League of Youth).

The Corporation Hotel stands on the site of what was Canton's largest farmhouse. It was here that Canton Market arose in 1859 and the first inn was the Market Hotel. The market was taken over by the Borough Council in 1875 and the splendid Corporation Hotel constructed in 1889. The hotel forms part of the imposing block of stone buildings, in the heart of Canton, which included the old post office and the Canton Carnegie library.

Canton Salvation Army members, *c.*1880. Cardiff was one of the earliest places visited by General William and Mrs Catherine Booth in their first mission after they had severed their association with the Methodist New Connexion in 1861. General Booth was invited to Cardiff after his mission to Cornwall in 1863. John and Richard Cory supported his work, contributing a share of the profits from one of their ships, which they had named the *William Booth*. The Salvation Army began its work in Canton in 1875, although it was another four years before the Canton Corps was launched officially, with its earliest barracks at what later became the YMCA in Wellington Street. Its first member was George Edwards, who had been attracted by the singing of some Stuart Hall members at an open air meeting in Riverside – which must have been lusty because he was sitting in Sophia Gardens at the time. He was converted that day and became the first sergeant-major of the Canton Corps. In those days the Salvation Army received a mixed reception, and violent animosity was not unusual: "Cardiff: Attacked by the Mob! Soldiers Wounded! Blood Shed!" ran a headline in a *War Cry* of 1880. But the 'Army' was not deterred by such opposition, which was offset by regional 'congresses', often held in Sophia Gardens, which could attract rapt audiences of up to 15,000. The Canton Band was formed in 1883, and included in its early members Joe Jones, 'The One-Eyed Drummer', who was renowned for giving his instrument a resounding thump and shouting 'Hallelujah' whenever he heard anything he appreciated. Gray and Halket (later Avon) streets often gave a rough time to the band, which was pelted with rubbish there. Between 1909 and 1913 the corps had no permanent premises and the band rehearsed in The Insole Arms, converting the landlord who then presented them with a drum. Meanwhile, the corps met in a dance hall above John & Sennington, ironmongers, on the corner of Severn Road. However, after Salem Chapel moved into its new church in 1910 (see p. 33), its former building in Albert Street became the Army's 'Citadel'. It remained so for the next 52 years.

The Very Revd Charles John Vaughan, DD, had been headmaster at Harrow before be became Dean of Llandaff, where he founded the Cathedral School in 1880. He considered that his most important work was training ordinands; he took these into his household and they became known as his 'Doves'. They included a future archbishop and seven bishops. At that time, Canton was the largest parish in Britain, and it was his favourite pastoral training ground. He took a special interest in St Catherine's Church, to which he and his wife each made a large contribution (of probably £1,000 each). His wife laid the foundation stone there, and it is said that the dedication of the church owes more to her than to the saint. His tomb in the Cathedral was sculpted by Sir William Goscombe John.

Lansdowne Road School was opened on 1 January 1898, and soon received its full (and startling) complement of 450 boys, 456 girls and 568 infants - a total of 1,474 pupils! During the First World War it served as a military hospital (see pp. 84-85) In 1984 the infants and junior departments combined, and a nursery school was opened there in 1995.

David Moore came to Canton from Bath in 1878 and ran his own horse-cab from Anglesey Street for over forty years. He carried many of Cardiff's well-known personalities, including Dr de Vere Hunt who took this photograph outside the Angel Hotel at the turn of the century. The fountain there was later removed.

Donald Knight's was one of the best known of the businesses in Cowbridge Road, well remembered for its wooden floors, cabinets of drawers, counters, curved-back chairs - and its traditional system of conveying money along overhead wires. It was founded in 1889 on the site of a present supermarket, and remained open until 1970; the family owned another business in Hereford.

ATLAS ENGINEERING WORKS,

CARDIFF.

MANUFACTURERS OF

Railway, Locomotive, Carriage and Wagon Wheels and Axles. Winby's Patent Corrugated Disc Wheels. Railway Iron and Steel, Straight and Cranked Axles. Marine and other Wrought Iron and Steel Shafts and Forgings. Iron, Brass and Steel Castings. Screw Propellers. Pit Wheels, Colliery Plant and Machinery. Single and Double Action Steam Hammers to 12 Tons Calibre. Rolling Mills and Machinery. Steam Engines and Boilers. Girders, Roofs, Tanks, Turntables, Cranes, Crabbs, Hoists. **Builders of Railway Wagons and every description of Railway Plant.** General Engineering Work.

ENGINEERS, IRON FOUNDERS AND FORGEMEN.

Atlas Terrace, Canton.

The Atlas Engineering Works was a hub of industry in Victorian Canton. It was situated on the south side of the bend in Atlas Road, and it may be one of its buildings which houses the present paper company there. Its manager was Frederick Winby, who lived in Canton Manor House in the period around 1873.

The Synagogue in Cathedral Road was opened in 1897 to serve the Jewish population of Cardiff, which had been increasing and which had outgrown its first place in worship in East Street (1858). It arose largely from the inspiration of Colonel Albert Goldsmid, whose home was at 'The Elms', Llandaff Road. Land for the development of the new synagogue was secured from the Marquess of Bute at a nominal rent. When the foundation stone was laid on 29 April 1896, Colonel Goldsmid welcomed the Christian guests and praised their faith which, he said, was 'spreading the knowledge of religion and morality and thus performing the Jews' mission for them'. More fellowship between the faiths was expressed at the opening ceremony on 12 May 1897, but this provoked the *Church Times* to rebuke the vicar of St Stephens for saying that 'the gospel could be preached in the new Synagogue as truly as in any Christian church'. Goldsmid replied in the Western Mail that he 'saw nothing incongruous in Christians assisting in the foundation of a synagogue in which their master had been wont to worship and preach' and went on to add that he himself had lent a hand for Christian denominational purposes without being less staunch to his race and faith. Membership of the Synagogue increased: in Edwardian times, another which had opened in Clare Road amalgamated with it, and later it was joined by a third which had arisen in Edwards Place. By the 1940s it had become known as 'The United Synagogue', and the observant life of Cardiff Jews would be centred there for some fifty years. However, their movement to the newly-built middle class suburbs of Cyncoed and Penylan led to the opening of a synagogue there in 1955. After that, the life of worship in Cathedral Road slowly ebbed away, and the Synagogue was closed and sold in 1989.

Plasturton Avenue and Gardens were developed by the Bute Estate around the turn of the century and made an elegant contribution to the Edwardian hey-day of Canton; the photograph above was taken in 1908. The family home of the sports' writer J.B.G. Thomas and his best-selling novelist son Craig was in this avenue, and the area attracted many in the media world after TWW (later Harlech Television) opened their Studios in Pontcanna Fields in 1958.

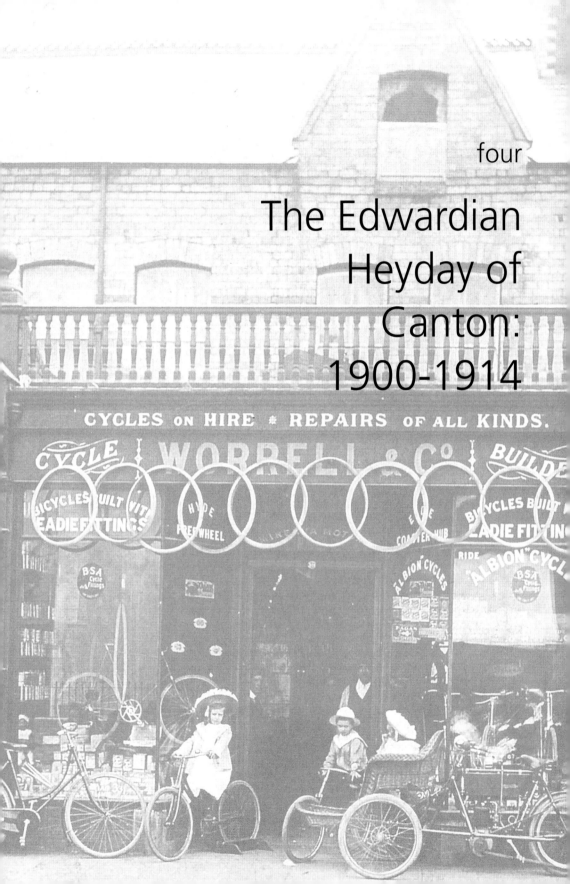

four

The Edwardian
Heyday of
Canton:
1900-1914

The first dozen or so years of the new century were perhaps Britain's hey-day, when the nation still felt secure, calm and superior and able to enjoy the fruits of its achievement before the onslaught of the First World War. Its image is often that of country-house parties, and indeed this was a golden age for the upper classes who spent their wealth more lavishly that their Victorian forebears would have allowed. The peerage began now to be infiltrated by the 'beerage', whose patronage of new developments like electricity and telephones led to them filtering down amongst the middle-class, who were also doing well – most of its members retained at least one servant. For the working-class, this was a time of hope, as social reform moved forward, the Labour Party was developing as a political force and the trade unions were becoming more powerful. For the first time almost everyone under forty had been taught the three 'r's in a regular school and this, together with the emergence of a popular press (circulation of the Daily Mail reached one million in 1901) ensured that there was increasing awareness of important issues. Seebohm Rowntree's study of York in 1899 confirmed Charles Booth's findings in his monumental study of social conditions in London, and showed that poverty was probably endemic. The Liberal Party was returned in an electoral upset in 1906 amidst a sense that social reform was overdue, and the new Prime Minister, Campbell-Bannerman spoke of making Britain 'less of a pleasure ground for the rich and more of a treasure house for the nation'. Reforms were introduced which opened the way to the welfare state: old-age pensions relieved the elderly from the fear of ending their lives in the workhouse, and compulsory state-aided insurance protected against illness. But by 1911, fifteen years of rising prices had brought a fall in real wages for the first time in two generations, and Britain was slowly losing its place as the 'Workshop of the World'.

The Western Mail welcomed the new century with the words that Wales was 'one of the brightest and most truly civilised spots in the Queen's dominion' which it attributed to 'the black mineral passing into the lap of Cardiff, Newport, Swansea and Llanelly, where the argosies of the nations await its arrival to convey it to the remotest parts of the earth'. A tribute in white Portland stone to the fortune and fame accumulated by Cardiff from that black mineral arose after the Corporation purchased Cathays Park in 1898 as the site for the new civic centre. Between 1901 and 1914 the University of Wales Registry, the City Hall and the Law Courts, the Glamorgan County Hall and the first part of the University College and of the Technical College all appeared in a parkland setting, and the foundation stone was laid of the National Museum of Wales. This became 'the finest town centre in Europe' and the creation of its splendid architecture, representing civil, regional and national institutions, contributed much to the success of Cardiff's petition for city status – which was granted on 23 October 1905. John Davies comments in A History of Wales that 'The confidence of the wealthy among the citizens of the new city was endless; with their huge banquets, their luxurious mansions and their appetite for honours, they were a notable part of the British capitalist class, which was then at the height of power and wealth'. The fourth, largest and last of the Bute Docks was opened by King Edward VII in 1907, and exports of coal continued to rise, to over 10 million tons in 1913 – which would prove to be the peak year in the industrial and commercial life of South Wales. This was probably Canton's hey-day too. Its growing pains were over and its people enjoyed much of the peace and prosperity of the time and of the town. There was, however, another side to the story and Canton has echoes of that, too. This was the time of 'the Great Unrest' when the unions were beginning to flex their new-found muscle – most turbulently in South Wales, where the miners had long-standing and justified grievances. This tension exploded most infamously in the Tonypandy riots of 1910 during which Colonel L.A. Lindsay – the Chief Constable of Glamorgan, whose headquarters were in Cowbridge Road – appealed to Winston Churchill for the assistance of soldiers.

Romilly Crescent near the junction with Severn Road in 1906, with Solomon Andrews' horse buses about to pass each other, Conway Road Methodist Church is in the distance. The row of shops on the left were run by Messrs Gibbs (draper), Bywater (ironmonger), Ellis (butcher) and Colley, who is recorded as a bootmaker in 1904; bootmaker and stationer in 1905 and, in the following year, 'Bootmaker, Stationer and Post office' – which was opportune, because in 1904 the Postmaster General had reported that the country was in the grip of a mania for postcards.

An Edwardian view of Neville Street. Between 1904 and 1920 the chapel on the far left was the home of one of the most unusual sects in Britain. The Catholic Apostolic Church was founded after some followers of the charismatic preacher Revd Edward Irving 'spoke in tongues' predicting the imminent apocalypse. The cult used elaborate ritual and ornament and appealed largely to the better-off. It spread to the continent and America, and claimed about fifty places of worship in Britain. Revd Irving died soon after being dismissed for heresy by the Presbyterian Church of Scotland in 1832, but the sect initiated by his followers continued for almost a century after.

At the top of Leckwith Hill in 1911. In the photograph are Mrs M.J. Johnston with her children Eileen and Jack, members of one of the older Canton families still resident in the area. A stroll to the bluebell woods on the hill was a favourite pastime of the past in Canton. It is said that on the way, a healing well was passed, from which cures have been claimed within living memory.

Mr & Mrs Ralph Jenkins in the drive of 'Chatsworth', No 55 Conway Road, 1911 with an early form of the motor-bike, a form of transport which would enjoy its golden age in the next decade; until 1928 there were more motor-cycles than cars in Wales. The first models were usually started with a run and a push from the driver, who then leapt on to the machine.

A tram at Canton cross-roads – the junction of Llandaff Road and Leckwith Road with Cowbridge
Road – in 1909. Davies the draper on the corner of Llandaff Road carried on until well after the First
World War, as did the Empire opposite, which was a greengrocer's and fruiterer's (not a cinema, as is
sometimes said).

Cowbridge Road near Cardiff (Canton) Bridge, around 1910. The houses on the left formed
Westbourne Crescent and Westbourne Place, and were demolished in 1971 and 1987 respectively. They
were replaced by the present Castlegate and Portcullis House developments.

The cosy Victorian nostalgia evoked by this scene of Cowbridge Road in the snow would not be enhanced by any hard facts.

An Edwardian view of Cowbridge Road looking towards the Corporation Hotel. The 'delta' is one of Canton's oldest features and probably held its first (and only) inn, long before The Cross shown in the photograph. Those premises are now occupied by the Midland Bank, but the projecting wooden corner ornament still remains.

A waggonette run by the cab proprietor James Redway is ready to move off from The Angel Hotel, Westgate Street, 1913. The business was operated from Lewis Court, behind the present Woolworths store in Canton. The court remained within living memory; in 1913 it consisted of nine small tenements which included a blacksmith and a wheelwright. At one time they were all served by one pump in the middle of the courtyard.

The Municipal Secondary School in Canton opened on 21 October 1907, and was the second in Cardiff. Later becoming Canton High School – motto *Semper Sursum* – it was transferred to new buildings in Fairwater in 1963 and was renamed Cantonian High School. Its former premises became the Chapter Arts Centre in 1971. This photograph was taken in the 1920s and shows the bell-tower lost when the building was damaged in the Blitz. The spire of St John the Evangelist can be seen in the background, while the shop on the corner of Market Place acted as the school 'tuck-shop'.

The altar of St Ann's chapel in the church of St Mary of the Angels (Llanfair yr Angylion), Kings Road. The 1,000 Roman Catholics in the Canton population of about 10,000 in the late 1860s were served by the Fathers of Charity as part of St David's parish. However, a school was opened in Wyndham Crescent on 13 June 1869, and this was used as a 'mass centre' until 'The Old Church' was built there around 1874. In 1877, St Mary's became a parish in its own right – the third oldest in Cardiff – under Father Louis Nedelic, author of *Cambria Sacra*, and in 1882 St Patrick's (Grangetown) became the first of its daughter churches. In 1897 the parish came under the care of the Benedictine Community at Ampleforth, and in 1901 an 'iron church' was erected in Kings Road. Four years later, Father Elphege Duggan was appointed to St Mary's, where he initiated much development before he died in 1921. The foundation stone of the present church was laid by Bishop Hedley on 20 January 1907. It was consecrated by him, in the presence of the Marquess of Bute, on 30 October of the same year – although it was not by then complete. The south aisle and other additions were finished in 1914, and the 'iron church' later became St Philip's, of the Church of England in Tremorfa. Father Duggan was followed by Father Ambrose Byrne, who is remembered as a spiritual inspiration to the parish. In his term the foundation stone of the new school was laid on 7 October 1928, and the tower of the church was opened on 11 February 1937. In 1926 the church of St Francis had become the second daughter church of St Mary's, and in 1936 St Clare's became the third. The church was damaged in the Blitz, and much rebuilding and redecoration took place. The new work was consecrated in 1953 in the presence of the Lord Mayor, Sir James Collins, who was a member of the parish. A favourite parish story tells how one of its priests had his bicycle stolen when visiting some of the poorer parts of the parish. He returned to St Mary's to ask for the intercession of St Anthony, the patron saint of things lost. On leaving the church he was astonished and delighted to find his bike resting outside. He rushed back in to say a wondrous thankyou, and came out a happy man – to find his bike stolen again!

George Coombs' hay and corn business, on the corner of Cowbridge Road and Albert Street, before the First World War. He was a city councillor and is remembered for handing out blue tickets which gave free admission to swimming baths for the children in the 1920s. The photograph below shows another shop of the same period, where George Huish sold fish and poultry.

Mathias' Yard in Cowbridge Road, *c*.1905, above. William Mathias built many of the houses in
Cathedral Road. His sons Thomas and William opened their yard in 1901 and began a business which
would last almost a century. Below is Minifie's bakery, *c*.1900. The business was at No 27 Severn Road,
next but one to the school (which can be seen) and to the tram depot which was on the site of the
present nursery school. Memories of the area's residents often recall the fumes from the soap factory in
Gray Street.

Above: the Cardiff Union Workhouse, *c.*1905 (see pp. 19 and 87). Below is an Edwardian view of the English Presbyterian Church in Cathedral Road which was built in 1903.

CATHEDRAL ROAD, CARDIFF.   No. 419.

Cowbridge Road, looking east from near the Kings Castle, c.1905. The solitary figure on the bicycle was actually one of a multitude, since this was the golden age of cycling. By the turn of the century bicycles had evolved into their modern form, and new models were being introduced almost every week. People realised that they were an easy and convenient means of getting about – but not always cheap, as the best models could cost the equivalent of £600 today. There were still ten million bicycles on the roads in the 1930s. The photograph below is of Clare Gardens in the same period. The streets in this area took their names from the Marcher Lords.

The fabled country-house parties of the Edwardian Age may have been rare in Canton, but the atmosphere of the period is conveyed in this photograph of a garden party held by St Luke's Church at Sophia Gardens in 1908.

The opening of the laboratory in Canton Secondary School, 1909. Those present included the Mayor and Mayoress, the headmistress (Miss Abbot), and the school's first headmaster, Mr Walter Brockington BA. He had previously been headmaster of Radnor Road School from its opening in 1888.

George Worrell's cycle shop at No 319 Cowbridge Road, *c.*1905. George and John Worrell's first trade was in Norfolk making and carving 'horses' for fairground rides. They came to Cardiff in 1902 and extended their business into bus and taxi operating, keeping abreast of developments in transport. By 1913 they had moved to larger premises at No 66 Cowbridge Road. George also appears in the photograph on page 84.

This early Edwardian photograph shows the parish church of St John the Evangelist finally complete. The side aisles had not been finished until five years after the first consecration of the nave in 1855; the spire was an addition of 1870; the chancel, organ chamber and vestry were ready in 1871; and finally the nave received an extra bay in 1902 to provide for the growth of the population. The surrounding hedge was removed when the grounds were renovated in 1984, in a scheme which won a Prince of Wales Award for providing the neighbourhood with a pleasant amenity. Since then the interior of the church has also been renovated.

Mrs David Lloyd George presenting prizes at Severn Road School on 22 December 1908. She was accompanied by Sir Alfred Thomas, MP for East Glamorgan, and chairman of the Welsh Parliamentary Liberal Party from 1897 to 1910. He became Lord Pontypridd in 1912.

Electric tram services in Cardiff began after the Mayor drove car No 1 along the Canton and Cathedral Road routes on 1 May 1902 and declared them open. Horse trams were withdrawn in the same year. The last tram made its final journey in 1950. The photograph shows Mr Charles Paull as driver of one of the 'Parks Express' trams which travelled between Victoria Park and Roath Park – it is pictured at the latter. Mr Paull spent a lifetime's service with the Corporation's transport department; he is seen earlier as a conductor on page 43.

Legislation in the 1870s began to secure independent financial rights for women, girls' schools and colleges began to appear, and, most importantly, women ratepayers were allowed to vote in the municipal elections of 1869. The cause was taken up most forcefully and famously by Emmeline Pankhurst, who started the Suffragette Movement in 1905. She claimed that the best political argument was a broken window-pane, and this photograph suggests that her followers agreed. It was taken outside Victoria Baptist Chapel on the corner of Eldon Street (Ninian Park Road) and Brunel Street in December 1913. As it turned out, their objective was finally achieved largely due to the participation of women in war work between 1914 and 1918. Women over thirty were first given the vote in the Representation of the People Act of 1918, and those between 21 and 30 received the franchise in 1928. One of the best-known suffragettes in Canton was the delightfully named Miss Rule, the headmistress of Radnor Road School in the 1930s; she lived in Romilly Road West..

Oposite below: This forerunner of the present Westgate Hotel was decorated for the coronation of King George V and Queen Mary on 22 June 1911. It was demolished in the redevelopment of the early 1930s, when the City Temple also arose alongside.

The two cinemas in Canton, in the 1960s and the 1920s. The first was the Coliseum (above) built in 1913. It was demolished in 1988 and replaced by the Castle Leisure Hall. The Canton Cinema, below, had appeared a year later in 1914 but disappeared two decades earlier when it made way for a series of supermarkets. The films they showed at first would have been silent. 'Talkies' came in 1927, with Al Jolson in *The Jazz Singer*, and they heralded the golden age of the cinema in the 1930s – already by 1925 more than half the population of Britain was going to the cinema at least once a week. In 1948 people still made 28 million visits a week, but the arrival of television caused this to slump to below three million by 1968.

five

The First World War and the Depression: 1914-1939

The First World War was not 'the war to end wars', but it did end much of the Victorian way of life and Britain's monopoly of world trade. Trade declined and unemployment rose from 1920 onwards, although from that date most manual workers received 'the dole'. Lloyd George, 'the architect of victory', was the first 'man of the people' to become prime minister, and the society he led was one in which many barriers had been broken down by the war. Membership of trade unions rose from over four million in 1914 to over eight million in 1925, and millions more working-class men were given the vote in 1918 – as were women over thirty, for the first time. The first-ever Labour Government took office in 1924, and effectively introduced council housing, but any further social reform was restricted by the Depression, which was greatly accelerated by the Wall Street crash of 1929. It hit hardest in areas of staple industries such as South Wales: 'the ten years from 1927 to 1937 represented the worst industrial depression South Wales has ever seen. Each of these years was to have been the last ...' and for the first time in generations emigration from South Wales exceeded immigration to the area. Unemployment in Merthyr reached 62 per cent in 1932, and in Maerdy the price of a house fell from £350 in 1920 to £50 in 1935. Cardiff, where unemployment rose to 25 per cent in 1930, would have suffered anyway due to its overdependence on the coal trade. Its docks never recovered after the First World War, by which time oil became the new preferred fuel and the best of the Welsh coal seams were worked out. Canton seems not to have suffered too badly, and indeed the local economy received an impetus when 350 semi-detached and better terraced houses were built around Victoria Park in the 1930s. Local trade also benefited from the construction of the large housing estate at Ely between 1928 and 1938. But several old established businesses closed along Cowbridge Road; numbers of unemployed men hired hand-carts to sell fruit and vegetables, and both the rugby club and the male choir here found it hard to keep going. Unemployment nationally reached its peak of 23 per cent in 1932, and began to fall in the following year. The large majority of the population remained in employment and, overall, real wages and standards of living rose between the wars. Those at work found that their labours were becoming less arduous, and there was more leisure time and many more ways in which it could be enjoyed. And there was a new lightness in the air, helped along by the ladies in their new-found enfranchisement. They had found that long dresses were unsuitable for their work in factory and farm during the war, and afterwards hemlines rose above the ground for the first time. By the 1920s skirts had risen almost to the knees and waistlines had dropped to the hips. Flesh colours replaced black for stockings, and more women began to wear lipstick and make-up. A new social life flourished to replace that which had previously been provided on almost every night of the week by churches and chapels: their attendances had begun to fall sharply after the war – perhaps because this four-year tragedy had raised too many hard questions. In Canton, the Dance Hall was run by Professor Sweeney above the Pavlova Billiard Room in Leckwith Road, and when this closed at 11 p.m., couples went on to St Luke's Hall where they could waltz on until 1 a.m.

Opposite below: Lansdowne Hospital served as a military hospital in the First World War and the photograph shows two Canadians and an Australian there. Annie Bishop (later Thomas) of Lionel Road helped at the hospital, with other members of the nearby St Luke's Church. She invited patients to write in an autograph book (which her daughter has kept) and two of the entries are shown on the previous page.

Right: Well-known Cardiff tailor Frank Jones, just before he left for the Somme. In that battle, his best friend, of the same name, was killed standing beside him. The horrific casualties of the Somme haunted Lloyd George, and were still in his mind when he later said of the Flanders' campaign: 'Divisions were sent in time after time to face the same slaughter in their ranks. And they always did their intrepid best to obey the fatuous orders'. Frank Jones ran a cutting room in St Mary Street, and also worked from his home in Llanfair Road. There he made clothes for many of the town's better-known people, including Solomon Andrews' son Arthur, who lived nearby in 'The Elms'. Mr Jones suffered injuries in the First World War, and in the Second World War lost two houses in South Morgan Street which were destroyed in the Blitz.

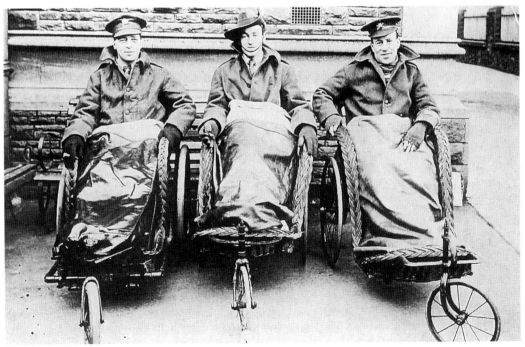

This is one of the first motor buses in Cardiff, operated by George Worrell from his premises in Cowbridge Road (see p. 77). Its route led from the Castle, along Cathedral Road and Palace Road to Llandaff North. The photograph was taken at the terminus there immediately after the First World War. The driver was Charles Thomas, who served afterwards as a driver with the Corporation for forty-four years. His brother Albert also worked for George Worrell, but later became the foreman at Romilly Motors in Romilly Crescent. The Cow and Snuffers public house can be seen in the background, where legend has it that Disraeli proposed to his wife Mary Ann, widow of Wyndham Lewis.

A chain-driven wagon, complete with hard tyres and oil lamps, c.1918. It was operated by the South Wales Jam & Marmalade Company, whose premises were on the probable site of Canton's medieval mill, at the bottom of Bassett Street. The company had been there since about 1888, and was managed by a Dugdale family who remained until c.1952. The site was previously occupied by Canton Flour Mill, which in 1875 was recorded as operated by D. Lougher of Canton Manor House.

These two aerial photographs were taken in 1930. The one above looks south-east towards the dockland, and is a good representation of the 'ride' through Pontcanna Fields – a fine feature in Canton, often overlooked. The tree-lined Cathedral Road runs parallel, close by. The lower photograph reveals the large size of the workhouse, with about twenty blocks which included a hospital, a chapel and, in earlier times, a night refuge. It was enlarged in 1881, and six years later held 1,870 inmates. There was also a side entrance in Kings Road, which at the time of the photograph led to the casual ward. The County Police headquarters can be seen near the centre, at the bottom of the photograph.

Mr and Mrs Sydney Herbert Rowland outside their home at No 127 Clive Road in 1915. Mrs Rowland, Sydney's second wife, was born in Fishguard and became a cook-housekeeper at Northumberland House in Cathedral Road. The three girls are, from left to right: Nora, aged about 8, Mary Faith, aged about 10 (the mother of Mrs Barbara Davies, who provided the photograph), and Elsie, who died of tuberculosis whilst training as a nurse in London. The trees lining Clive Hill accounted for its familiar name of 'Shady Hill'.

Sydney Rowland, outside his shop on Cowbridge Road, late 1920s. He began as a painter and decorator working from home, and later entered into partnership with Robert Trapnell. Trapnell's was a well-known ironmonger's business which survived on the corner of Picton Place (the present site of 'Boot's the Chemist') until the 1960s.

The Canton Juvenile Prize Choir in 1926, conducted by Madam Gwenllian Williams. Madam Gwenllian was the mother of Miss Eira Williams, who has conducted both the Novello Singers (which flourished for almost fifty years), and the Snowflakes Choir; each broadcast regularly. The latter choir is shown in the photograph on page 109.

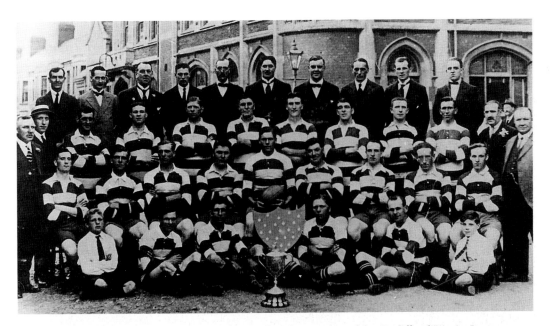

Canton RFC, 1920-21 season. The club was a founder-member of the Cardiff and District League. Initiated in the 1880s, the team has been regularly successful in the Mallett Cup (which is the oldest of the Welsh District cups). Its record of trophies is hard to equal, as is its achievement in 1907, when the side won all its matches. Many of its members have gone on to play in 'first-class' rugby. In 1989 the club obtained its first clubhouse at Lawrenny Avenue which was opened by David East, then Secretary of the Welsh Rugby Union.

Above: Pope's sweet shop, c.1910. Mr A. Pope opened his first sweet shop at James Street in the 1890s. About 1910 he opened a second shop at No 227 Cowbridge Road, where he also made sweets, to the delight of children of all ages who watched the process with fascination. The James Street shop was closed in the 1920s, and Mr Pope concentrated his trade at Cowbridge Road until he retired (and his shop closed) in 1937. Meanwhile, from 1924 his son Charles had taken part of his father's shop to sell photographic equipment. In 1925 the son opened his own shop at No 235 Cowbridge Road offering photographic and fancy goods; these premises had previously been Barclays Bank, and the old bank counter is still in use today. Charles retired in 1965, and was succeeded by his son Dennis, who now runs the oldest photographic shop in Cardiff. He is assisted by his daughter Deborah, who is the fourth generation of the family in the business. Below: Peacocks store in the 1930s. The Canton branch of this Midlands company has always enjoyed a popular reputation for providing a wide range of merchandise at competitive prices.

It was the policy of this company, founded in the 1920s, to sell food at the lowest prices, and its trade soared in the Depression of the next decade. The photograph shows Candle King's premises in Cowbridge Road opposite Albert Street; there was also a store on the other side of the main road, and branches throughout the city.

The May Day horse show in Sophia Gardens, 1927. At that time, motor transport was beginning to come into its own, but horse-drawn vehicles remained on the roads until well after the Second World War. Their owners took pride in presenting them at their best for the horse show, which was always well attended and hence completely threw into chaos the streets around Sophia Gardens. The photograph shows the entry from W.E. Dyke, the fruiterer and greengrocer from Kings Road.

Taken in the same year as the photograph above, this is a good example of the competition that the horse-drawn vehicle was then facing. It was one of several vehicles run by the Cardiff Dairy Company from their premises on the corner of Atlas Road and Thurston Street. Charles Banwell was the proprietor.

Above: James Clarke with one of his first horse-drawn vehicles, *c.*1910. James Clarke came to Cardiff from Somerset around 1890. He began his haulage business from Coke Street (later named Kingston Road) but soon moved to Glynne Street, from where he built up a fleet of six horse-drawn waggons which usually carried fruit and provisions around Cardiff. However, he also provided a daily service to Barry, which needed a 'cock' horse at the bottom of each of the two hills en route. His first motor vehicles were acquired from a sale of army equipment at the site of the slaughter house and market in Market Road. Later be built up a fleet of eight vans, ranging from two-and-a-half 'tonners' up to a furniture lorry. These enabled him to extend his deliveries into the valleys. His son Sydney continued the business until he was prompted to sell it by the nationalisation of transport in 1947. The photograph below shows James with his fleet of vans in Glynne Street, as they prepared for a Whitsun treat in 1925.

Chancery Lane, decorated for the coronation of King George VI in 1937. This is one of a group of streets whose names derive from the legal profession: Littleton, Lyndhurst, Mansfield, Chancery and – previously, before they were demolished or received a new name – Blackstone, Coke and Eldon streets.

The Atlas Hotel changed its name to The Ninian Park Hotel in the early 1920s, which was the golden decade for Cardiff City AFC. The club won promotion to the First Division immediately after joining the Football League in 1920. In 1924 its team almost won the First Division Championship, and it reached the cup final in the following year; the crest was reached in 1927 when Cardiff City defeated Arsenal 1-0 to win the FA Cup. The Ninian Park Hotel was demolished in 1978, not long after this photograph was taken.

The railway crossing leading to Thomas Owen's Paper Mill in 1932. Behind the far gate, on the right, can be seen the small green wooden 'coffee house' which stood there from 1912 until 1937. For the last ten of those years it was run by A.J. Taylor. From then until about 1949 it was 'Jack's Transport Cafe'. The Ely Paper Works' Institute was near the opposite corner.

Corporation buses conveying guests to the opening of Leckwith viaduct by Leslie Hore-Belisha, Minister of Transport, 17 April 1935. Motor transport began to be commonplace in the 1930s – it had already increased six-fold between 1921 and 1929 – and new or improved roads were needed. The viaduct replaced a medieval bridge, and the Western Avenue was constructed on the other side of Canton in the same decade.

'Billy the Seal' was found in 1912 by Mrs Bugg of Conway Road, in a box of fish off a Neale & West trawler on its return from the Irish coast. He was given a home in Victoria Park and remained there until 1939. Stories about him are legion; they include reports of him escaping in the floods of 1927 and venturing into town, from whence he returned, tired, on a tram; and 'Fishy' Evans of Telford Street is reputed to have taken him out on his fish round as a 'trade-mark'. His death in 1939 was reported on the front page of the *South Wales Echo* with the words: 'Billy is dead but will not be forgotten by all who knew him'. Now celebrated in a song by Frank Hennessey, Billy sprang one last surprise: the National Museum of Wales included his skeleton in their osteological collection, and confirmed that Billy was in fact a female seal – and would have been better named Milly.

An Edwardian view of the monkey-house in Victoria Park. This was only one of several compounds making up a menagerie along the west side of the park. It held parrots and peacocks, smaller animals such as guinea-pigs, rabbits and a pole-cat and, near the entrance from Romilly Road West, goats and a wallaby. These could all be seen in the 1920s and early 1930s.

The railway crossing on the main London-West Wales line, Leckwith Road, early 1930s. The view looks north towards Cowbridge Road, and the present Ninian Park Hotel stands on the site of the three-storey house. There was havoc here when crowds spilled out from Ninian Park football ground, around the corner, and came to closed gates. There were three other crossings over the main line through Canton before the tracks were raised; at the paper mill, the sanatorium, and at the bottom of Bassett Street.

A Swansea-Cardiff train passing the paper mill on 3 November, 1927. After those floods, which began two days earlier, the Council straightened the course of the River Ely and undertook other work which prevented their recurrence. In St Luke's Church a tide-mark can still be seen which records the height of the water there: 2 feet, 4 inches.

Mrs Chick, the first and last of the 'Flower Sellers of Gray Street'. The people of Gray Street were harder hit than most by the Depression. With typical ingenuity, they devised various means of alleviating the hardship, and one has entered into the folklore of Canton. Mrs Norah Chick took to filling her pram with flowers, which she sold around the streets. The idea was a success, several of her neighbours followed suit, and the flower sellers of Gray Street entered local history. It was not unknown for local couples, also victims of the Depression, to buy the flowers for their wedding from Mrs Chick. She enjoyed her new found trade so much, and it became so popular, that she continued long after the Depression had come to an end.

Edgar Harding, with his son Desmond, outside his shop at No 391 Cowbridge Road in 1962. Edgar opened his shop in 1930, during the Depression which was causing the closure of other businesses. The story, not denied by his son, is that he began with one bicycle in the window. When asked for a tyre, he sold one off the display and bought two more at trade prices. He did the same when asked for a chain. And so he built up his business, which was taken over by his son and lasted for almost fifty years.

A party at Picton Place to celebrate the coronation of King George VI and Queen Elizabeth on 12 May 1937. Picton Place was one of the streets within the triangle formed by Cowbridge Road, Wellington Street and Leckwith Road. It was demolished in the 1960s, with the others: Albert Street (north), East Street, Mary Ann Street and North Morgan Street.

A party in Gray Street to celebrate the Coronation in 1937. It was here that Sir William Goscombe John (see p. 25) was born in 1860, and the street remained at the heart of the community in Canton. During the first quarter of the nineteenth century, it contained Taylor's Bone and Soap Factory, next door but one to The Bird in Hand public house. It was demolished in the 1960s to make way for a car park.

Clive Hall, near the top of Clive Hill, was built around 1880 for William Pearson Price, who owned a firm of clothiers, hatters, hosiers and outfitters in St Mary Street. Mrs Olive Rex founded Clive Hall School there in 1926, after failing to find a suitable school for her daughter Rosalind. It began with six on the register (including her daughter) and flourished, so that by 1962 190 pupils were being taught here. The school closed in 1987, and the hall was taken over by Monkton House School.

The knife-grinder 'Mr Flindo' in the 1930s. His cart was made by Jack Verallo, a popular ice-cream seller in Canton during the same decade. The variety of street traders included those whose trade was in whitelime, shrimps, hot-cross buns and fresh rolls and, of course, 'old iron' – the 'rag-and-bone man'. Their 'street cries' were so much a part of life that a recording of them has been made.

Cardiff Motor School, run by A.J. Pitman at No 363 Cowbridge Road in 1932. The first British car for the popular market was the Austin Seven, which cost £225 when it was introduced in 1922; its price had been brought down to £118 by 1932. But this was only the beginning of popular motoring. The total of one million private cars on the roads in the previous year meant that they were owned by only one family in ten.

Children at Radnor Road School take part in a pageant as part of their St David's Day (Dydd Gŵyl Dewi) eisteddfod in 1925.

Philip Harding began his business in 1928 at No 210 Cowbridge Road, next to the newsagent Luther James. Like many others during the Depression, he put his hand to whatever might increase his trade. He employed his former coach-trimming skills and, as his wife was a member of the Grimwade family, he also sold second-hand goods. He survived the slump, and in 1951 his son Cliff, with his wife Freda, started in business by taking up one of his windows to sell china. The photograph shows Philip around 1954, when one of their 18-piece teasets cost ten shillings and sixpence. His grandson John extended the business in 1985 by opening at premises in No 226, previously occupied by Rosemary the florist and Link's the fruiterer. Together, the Harding family make up one of the oldest and most popular of the small businesses in Cowbridge Road. Below is the branch of the Home and Colonial Stores in Cowbridge Road at the time Philip Harding was entering business.

Kathleen and Harry Hichens on the pier at Weston, not long before their marriage in 1940. Latterly, Harry has become well known by providing facilities for pensioners in Canton. He raised most of the funds to refurbish the Slade Hall and organised a series of popular regular functions. Like Father Bevanot (p. 116), Harry and Kath became a familiar sight in Canton on their bicycles in their ninth decade. Their cycling began with a tandem fitted with a sidecar for their children and their bikes have taken them to France, Holland and Belgium.

Harry became a convenor whilst working in the aircraft section at Curran's during the war, and usually took a bold and unequivocal stand in union affairs. The media as far afield as Australia watched him with bated breath in 1971, when he protested against what he thought was an unfair strike settlement. For five days he sat alone atop a 70-foot water tower. The management tried several ruses to get him down. A safety inspector was sent up: 'Which country in Britain has the worst safety record?' asked Harry. 'Wales', was the reply. 'Which town in Wales?'... 'Cardiff'...'And which plant in Cardiff?'...'This one'. 'Aye', said Harry, 'and I'm safer up here than I am down there'. Twenty-six years employment with the firm thus came to an abrupt end.

St. Winifride's Hospital, Romilly Crescent, Cardiff

The Congregation of the Sisters of the Sacred Hearts of Jesus and Mary was founded in 1866 by Father Victor Braun to help delinquent young girls in Paris. The caring work of its sisters soon included nursing, and was brought to Britain with the opening of a home in London. An orphanage was built in Rothesay by Lady Bute and the order began to provide education and accommodation for mentally handicapped children. It was for this work that the Queen bestowed the OBE upon the Mother Superior General in 1955. The Sisters came to Canton in 1928, when the Lord Ninian Hospital was opened in Cathedral Road. This had been the bequest to them from Lady Bute in memory of her son, who was killed in the First World War. A neighbour could remember there the old custom of doorknockers being muffled to prevent heavy banging disturbing patients – an effect which others with sick relatives achieved by wrapping sacking around the knocker. St Winefride's was built by the order in 1938, after its premises in Cathedral Road proved too small. It served as a private surgical hospital until 1986, when it became a nursing home for the elderly, sick and terminally ill. In 1978 its work was extended by the Jane Hodge Residential Home for the Elderly (situated within its grounds and fronting Conway Road), arising from the generosity of Sir Julian Hodge in memory of his mother. Canton is served by members of two other congregations of sisters; those of the Sisters of Charity, and the Sisters of St John of God. They care for the deaf, and teach, respectively.

six

Second World War and Recovery: 1939-1960

Between 1939 and 1945, families here suffered in the same way as those throughout the land, with men away at war. But Canton had its own particular hardships to endure, and these came to a head on the night of 2 January 1941, when an air raid killed 156 in the city. Riverside suffered from air raids more than any other part of the town, and that night is especially remembered for the loss of an entire funeral party at Blackstone Street, which was not rebuilt after the war. It was the same raid that damaged Canton Secondary School, the timber yard in North Morgan Street, Llandaff Cathedral and Canton Cinema – where those who were there remember with a smile that the film showing was Night Train to Munich (starring Margaret Lockwood and Rex Harrison). Canton survived, and did so with a spirit which the Chief Constable used as an example of 'the calm way in which the public treated the worst efforts of the German fire-bombers, when three incendiary bombs fell onto a suburban cinema and dropped in flames into the crowded auditorium. There was no sign of panic, and the people seated nearby merely moved away while members of the staff extinguished the bombs. They then returned to their seats, and the show went on – not a single person left the building'. Later, the King and Queen visited Cardiff and paid tribute to its citizens with the words: 'Tis not the walls that make the city, but the people who live within them'. A fear that the end of hostilities would see a repeat of the hard times that followed the First World War was not realised, and after a few years of austerity and rationing Britain entered a period of prosperity. In many people's minds the 1950s was the best decade since the nation's Victorian heyday, and there were visions of a new and golden Elizabethan Age. Indeed, there was much to give encouragement, both nationally and locally; when the Welsh former coal-miner Aneurin Bevan implemented the Beveridge report in 1946 he created the Welfare State, which would soon be perceived as taking care of everyone 'from the cradle to the grave'; a year later the Earl of Plymouth presented St Fagans Castle to the National Museum of Wales – it would become one of the finest folk museums in the world, attracting 250,000 visitors in 1990 – and in the same year, the 5th Marquess of Bute presented the Castle and Sophia Gardens to the City of Cardiff. By 1951 Britain felt confident enough to mount a small-scale replica of the triumphant Great Exhibition of 1851, and the Festival ship Campania visited Cardiff. National optimism seemed euphoric at the coronation of Queen Elizabeth II on 2 June 1953, a day after Hilary's conquest of Mount Everest which was hailed as 'the crowning glory'; in 1955 Cardiff became the capital city of Wales, and three years later hosted the British Empire and Commonwealth Games – where Howard Winstone won a Gold Medal for Wales in the boxing tournament held at Sophia Gardens Pavilion. At the closing ceremony the Queen announced that henceforth Prince Charles would be known as 'The Prince of Wales' and the crowds responded with the only song possible. There seemed to be solid grounds for optimism at that time, too: before long, three-quarters of the population would be better off than before the war, and two out of every five families would be living in post-war homes. Macmillan might well say that we had 'never had it so good'.

Canton, too, shared in the sense of well-being of the time. Housing losses of the war years were made good, and there was a pleasant development of 124 semi-detached houses around Broadhaven. Some new light industry and commerce appeared, and with the end of rationing the shops along 'the front' in Cowbridge Road took on a new lease of life. But in hindsight the end of the fifties was the end of an era, and from the sixties onwards life would take a different course - the community around Wellington Street, for example, would be torn apart by redevelopment. The fifties saw the end of far more than just the horse and cart, the pitch-and-toss and horse sales of the gypsies opposite Ninian Park on Sundays. For the time being, however there was a warm glow that not even the fuel shortage and snow of 1947 could freeze out.

AIR RAID PRECAUTIONS

IN CASE OF INJURY

Wounded and gas contaminated casualties who can walk should go direct to the nearest First Aid Post. If you suspect that your clothing has been contaminated by liquid gas, remove the affected garment immediately and place it outside the house, then wash yourself thoroughly Stretcher cases will be taken to hospitals

GAS MASKS

TAKE CARE OF YOUR GAS MASK. Learn how to put it on and take it off and how to store it properly. Keep it ready for immediate use. If you have no gas mask or if your mask does not fit or seems out of repair, speak to your Warden about it at once.

LIGHTING RESTRICTIONS

All windows, doors, skylights or openings which would show a light, must be screened so that no light can be seen from outside Do not use a light in a room unless the blind or curtain is drawn, and remember that a light at the back of the house is just as visible from the air as one at the front.

AIR RAID WARNING SIGNALS

● WARNING SIGNAL   *Warbling or intermittent sound on siren, Whistles blown by police and wardens* ● GAS WARNING *Rattles sounded.* ● RAIDERS PASSED   *Continuous sound on siren* ● ALL CLEAR *Handbells rung*
When you hear the WARNING Signal TAKE COVER AT ONCE and stay there until you hear the continuous sound on the siren

or the ringing of a handbell. Have your Gas Mask with you. If RATTLES have been used warning you of gas, do not come out until you hear HANDBELLS.

FIRE PRECAUTIONS

Be ready to deal with an incendiary bomb. Clear all lumber from your attic NOW, and see that you have easy access to the attic or roof space. Provide two buckets filled with water and, if possible, a stirrup hand pump with two-purpose nozzle, either producing spray for dealing with the bomb itself, or producing a jet for tackling the resulting fire.
Have a reserve supply of water in buckets or tubs. Leave used water in bath.
If you have no stirrup hand pump, have two buckets of sand or dry earth near the top of the house, and a shovel with a long handle for putting sand on the bomb. After covering the bomb with sand place it in a bucket which has a few inches of sand in the bottom, and remove it from the house. Scrape up every particle of burning metal. The resulting fire will then have to be extinguished. Buckets of water or a folded blanket kept wet from a bucket of water might be used.
On no account throw water on the bomb or an explosion may result

If you cannot put out the fire send for help to

★ **HANG THIS CARD IN A PERMANENT AND PROMINENT POSITION**

61—6782

When Mrs Elaine Laanemets, of Riverside, experienced her first air raid, she said: 'Then I knew we were at war'. The Home Front was as important, and often as bloody, as any other. With the Blitz, Hitler tried and failed to break the will of the British people. A large, and largely unsung, part of our defence relied upon the work of the ARP; the notice explains procedures around Romilly Road in the event of an air raid.

These two photographs record some of the damage caused in Canton by air raids. The one above shows the corner of Lansdowne Road and Wembley Road after the raid on 18 May 1943. Fifty bombers flew unusually low, taking advantage of the fact that the anti-aircraft guns on Ely racecourse were out of action. One strafed a munitions train, leaving pock-marks which can still be seen on the bridge at Sanatorium Road. Forty-five people were killed on this the last night on which bombs fell upon Cardiff. The photograph below shows the scene around the Conservative Club in Neville Street after the raid on 2 January 1941. Local people retained their sense of humour, even at the worst times. One man trying to hurry a neighbour into a shelter was told to wait whilst she found her false teeth: 'Never mind those, Hitler's dropping bombs, not sandwiches', he shouted.

VE Day celebrations in Avon Street, May 1945. The war in Europe came to an end with the total surrender of German forces on 8 May 1945. The war in the Far East, however, continued until an atomic bomb dropped upon Hiroshima on 6 August 1945 precipitated the surrender of Japan. Victory over Japan (VJ) was celebrated on 15 August and further street parties were held despite food rationing, which did not end completely until 1950.

The 1950s was the last period in which many of the traditional games were popular. Not the least of the many causes for their disappearance was the fact that increasing traffic made street games too dangerous. Those that began to vanish included hide-and-seek, rat-tat-ginger, hopscotch, skipping ropes from pavement to pavement, gobs (fivestones) and bombarino. The above picture shows some Canton children with their bogie which was made out of a few planks and a set of wheels from a pram.

Gypsies on Leckwith Common, *c.*1941. The Romanies were regular visitors to Canton. Their womenfolk, usually wearing a shawl and often smoking a clay pipe, would sell pegs and nick-nacks from house to house. It is often said that they expected their palms to be crossed with silver (a 'tanner' would do in fact), and threatened a curse if disappointed. But other recollections speak of them more kindly. They chose St John's Church for their funerals, which were colourful events followed by a procession of twenty or more caravans.

A tram approaching Victoria Park in the early 1940s. In the background can be seen Mathews' ice cream parlour in Victoria Park Road East. Just around the corner, in Cowbridge Road, was the Trico. It offered take-away ice-cream and a vast array of sweets to children on their way to the park.

Hilda Banwell and her accordion band, 1940. Miss Banwell taught music from her home on the corner of Romilly Road and Preswylfa Street. During the war her band entertained munitions workers; afterwards it performed mostly for charity. Miss Banwell was an able teacher with a waiting-list of pupils. These included Mario Conway, who went on to win national prizes for his accordion playing.

The Snowflakes Juvenile Choir, winners of first prize in their class at the National Eisteddfod held in Mountain Ash in 1946. Many of the former Snowflakes singers went on to join the Gwenllian Singers, still conducted by Miss Eira Williams who has made a rich and unique contribution to the musical life of the capital city from her home in Cowbridge Road East (see also p. 89).

The Canton Cinema in the 1950s. It is remembered from this decade for the 'tanner rush' on a Saturday morning, when children flocked to pay either sixpence or ninepence to watch a programme of cartoons and films. The occasional breakdown of a film would be greeted with a thunder of feet stamping. Adult prices for the regular performances were two shillings or one shilling and sixpence.

Sophia Gardens Pavilion was the 'Earls Court' of South Wales. It was opened in 1951 and survived until the roof collapsed in a snowstorm on 2 January 1982, leading to the demolition of the building in February of the following year. It held a variety of events including 'Ideal Home Exhibitions', concerts, and sports tournaments, and was visited by many top stars including Danny Kaye and Tommy Steele.

Revd Ivor Cassam, BA, BD was born at Treherbert in 1916 and educated at University College, Cardiff. He became minister at New Trinity in 1948, when the induction prayer was offered by Revd Dr Howell Elvet Lewis ('Elfed'), who had officiated at the induction of the first minister there in 1894. New Trinity had built up its congregation strongly after the war, and reached its largest ever membership in Revd Cassam's ministry, during which the first lady deacon was elected. Ecumenically-minded, he instituted joint Free Church services in Canton, and in his term New Trinity founded churches in Fairwater and Llanishen. A frequent guest-speaker in both English and Welsh throughout Wales, he wrote regularly for the press and also conducted a series of radio broadcasts. One of his foremost early interests was in the Mission to the Deaf and Dumb, and his desire to exercise a ministry in social work led to him resigning the pastorate in 1960 and becoming Director of the Council of Social Service for Wales.

Bill Winton was born in 1912 at Merthyr Tydfil, where he was the first boy from the County School to win an Under-18 Welsh rugby cap. Completing his education at St David's College, Lampeter, Jesus College, Oxford, and St Michael's, Llandaff, he soon found himself with the forces after entering the ministry, and was mentioned in dispatches. In 1949 he was appointed Rector of St John's, and a lasting memorial to his work in Canton was the building of the Church Hall in Leckwith Road. In 1966 he moved to the parish of Whitchurch, where he stayed until his retirement. He was made a canon of Llandaff Cathedral, and awarded the MBE for services to the Territorial Army. He was also one of the principal driving forces behind the foundation of the Bishop of Llandaff School, of which he became the Chairman of Governors.

Orchard Place celebrates the Festival of Britain and the visit of the Festival ship, *Campania* to Cardiff in 1951. The cake was made by Mrs Anne Harrison, on a superstructure built by a former seaman on the *Ark Royal* – most appropriate since the *Campania* was a converted aircraft-carrier.

Two trolleybuses at the junction of Lower Cathedral Road and Neville Street in the 1960s. The first of the trolleybuses ran in 1942 and their service came to end in 1970.

Right: Revd David Davies was educated at Radnor Road School and found his faith at the nearby Gospel Hall in Llandaff Road. In 1934 he travelled to China as an evangelist and medical missionary, and worked there with Gladys Aylward. In 1940 he was captured by the Japanese, who accused him of being a spy and tortured him throughout the next five years. He returned to Britain after the war, and served as the Presbyterian minister of three churches in the Rhymney Valley. He retired to Canton, and died in 1978. His biography, *Born to Burn* was published in 1972.

Below: Party in Avon Street to celebrate the coronation of Queen Elizabeth II on 2 June 1953. The boy in the centre is Peter Rodrigues, who would later become a professional footballer and captain of Southampton AFC when they won the FA Cup in 1976.

An aerial view over Canton in 1962. Lansdowne Road runs along the bottom of the photograph, Victoria Park is in the bottom left corner, and Pontcanna Fields reach across the top of the view. It shows well how much greenery Canton has around, and within it.

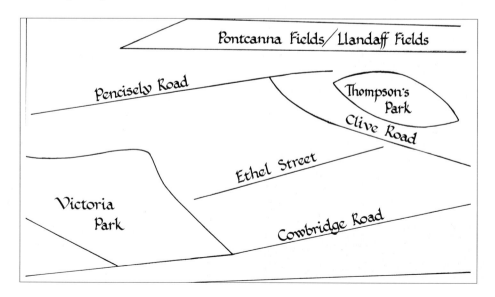

Craig Thomas was born 24 November 1942, the son of sports writer, J.B.G. Thomas and his wife Gwen of Plasturton Avenue. Educated at Radnor Road School, Cardiff High School and University College, Cardiff, he obtained a Master's Degree in English and took up teaching at Lichfield. He still lives there with his wife, Jill. His first novel, *Rat Trap* was published in 1976, and his second, in the following year, was *Firefox* which was made into a film starring Clint Eastwood. He has since written a sequence of novels, all of them best-sellers.

Dom Laurence Bevenot is typically remembered 'cycling merrily and perilously round the City well into his ninth decade', as the *Daily Telegraph* remarked in his obituary. He was, however, best known as the choirmaster at Ampleforth for twenty-five years, and as a pioneer in the revival of plain-chant in the Roman Catholic Church in England. He composed a number of hymns and several masses, and also wrote two successful music-dramas for Canterbury Cathedral. Stone-carving and lettering were a secondary interest. A member of a family of scholars, this 'gentle, sensitive and lovable man' served as a priest at St Mary's in Kings Road for 26 years until his death in 1990, aged 89. A composition of his work has been included on a collection of Gregorian chant from Ampleforth released recently by Classic FM.

In the 1970s the *South Wales Echo* reported that Mrs Margaret Wilson was the last resident of Harvey Street, crossing the end of Glamorgan Street, where she had lived for seventy years. Best-known as 'Aunt Maggy' to everyone in the area, Mrs Wilson said: 'I haven't got a bath, so I have a good scrub down in the tin tub, and if I want any hot water I boil the kettle. It's not too bad, but the toilet is down the yard and I don't like going out there at night. The stairs are rickety, but I've got a rope to help me get down them. I only pay £3.98 a fortnight in rent, so I suppose I can't grumble'. The Housing Director said that the population in Canton had got deep roots in the area, and that a flat had been found for Mrs Wilson in nearby Railway Terrace.

The Duke of York, on the corner of Wellington Street and Albert Street, not long before it closed in 1975. The other public houses of Wellington Street included The Red Cow, Rover Vaults, The Swan and The Greyhound.

Albert Street (north), not long before it was demolished in the redevelopment of the area that spanned the 1960s and 1970s. The novelist Howard Spring was born at No 32 Albert Street.

Cowbridge Road in the snow of 1965. Zeidmen's, the draper's, can be seen on the corner of Severn Road, in the premises soon to be occupied by the ironmongery business of John & Sennington.

The staff of Canton High School for Boys in 1947-8 included from right to left, back row: W. Cork, W. Waters, B. Watson, T. Dowse, D. Arwyn Jones, R.W. Lewis, D.W. Sims, W.G. Thomas, Russell Jones, M.G. Jenkins, D. Holley, E.J. Brook, E. Richards and J.C. Bates. Front row: C. Newberry, P.T. Griffiths, R.F. Caulkwell, G. Cleal, R.S. Devonald, A.B. Davies, Elwyn Jones (Headmaster), G.L. Davies, J. King, S. Crammer, T. Edwards, N. Smith, and P.L. Emery.

Councillor Bella Brown being presented to Her Majesty the Queen in 1978. The Lord Mayor on this occasion was the Rt. Hon. Dorothy Lewis, the Riverside councillor from whom the Dorothy Lewis Home in Canton has taken its name.

The Rt. Hon. Bella Brown, Lord Mayor of Cardiff, 1979-80. She is wearing the chain of office purchased by the Corporation to commemorate the coming-of-age of the 3rd Marquess of Bute. Mrs Bella Brown served as a councillor for Canton between 1959 and 1987. She became Lord Mayor in 1979-80, and chairman of South Glamorgan County Council in the following year. 'Bella', as she is always known, has been one of the most popular of all the Canton councillors, and her surgery on Friday evenings at her family home in Theobald Road was always well attended. One brother, Trevor, was also a local councillor, and a second, Thomas, became Mayor of Dar-es-Salaam; he had remained in Tanganyika after being stationed there with the RAF in the Second World War.

Cowbridge Road in the snow of 1947. 'The Candle King' can be seen on the right, opposite Albert Street. The snow of that year was the worst since 1894, and was accompanied by a fuel shortage. Families hauled prams to coal sidings to collect whatever might be available and when coal ran out it was replaced with fuel blocks purchased from shops. In those days, before central heating was common, most people relied upon coal fires for warmth.

Sparkes' Garage in Penhill Road, 1950s. The site is now occupied by Penhill House, of recent naming and not to be confused with the medieval – and still remaining – Penhill House in Llandaff Road. The garage was a short distance from 'The White Shop' on the corner of Conway Road, owned for many years by the Tyrrell family.

Cowbridge Road in the floods of 5 December 1960. The water did not abate for several days and boats were brought in from Roath Park lake to provide the most convenient means of transport.

O'Dare's kiosk beside the railway bridge in Leckwith Road, in the early 1930s. It was in the house of the owners, Mr & Mrs O'Dare that Viscount Tonypandy – then George Thomas – received his first nomination as a parliamentary candidate for the Cardiff Central constituency.

St Mary's rugby team, 1955-6 season. The priest is Dom Gabriel Gilbey, who is perhaps the only Roman Catholic curate to sit in the House of Lords. A member of the family of wine and spirit merchants, he later inherited the title Baron Vaux of Harrowden. Several members of this team went on to play 'first-class' rugby, including Tony Hurford (Newport), Philip Walsh (Neath) and Terry O'Gorman (Glamorgan Wanderers).

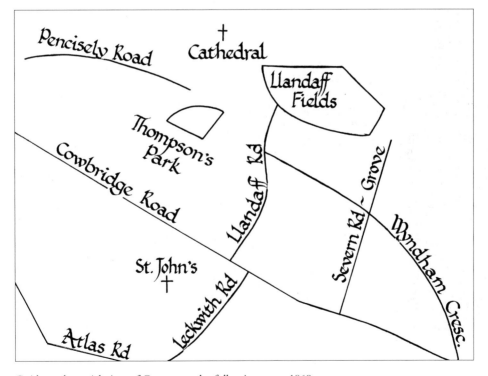

Guide to the aerial view of Canton on the following page, 1969

The Salvation Army Band in Chancery Lane, 1950s. The Canton Corps is one of five in Cardiff, and its music is provided by the Senior Band, the Junior Band, the Songsters' Brigade (of mixed adults) and the Singing Company (of juniors) – supplemented occasionally by a timbrel group. They would not claim it for themselves, but general opinion is that the Canton Band is the best in South Wales.

Canton from the air in 1969, looking north from the railway depot. The best marker is the parish church of St John the Evangelist, surrounded by its circle of dark trees and hedge.

Margaret Lockwood at the Canton Male Voice Choir's annual dinner in 1955. She made a presentation to mark the 50 years that Charlie Griffiths had sung with the choir. The group was formed in 1898 at The Old Barley Mow public house in Cowbridge Road, and since then has given more than two thousand performances. It reached one of its peaks in the 1920s, beginning with a sold-out concert in 1920 attended by an audience of almost a thousand people. In the next decade, bookings came in from the Park Hall and the old Hippodrome in Westgate Street. The Blitz, however, destroyed the entire music stock and most of the records, but the choir survived and adopted the new name Cardiff (Canton) Male Voice Choir in the early 1950s.

Canton RFC, 1957-8 season. This has a reputation as a 'family club', well illustrated by this photograph which shows four members of the same family: David, Des and Peter Roblin as players, and Lyn Roblin as secretary. John Roblin would have been there too, but he was playing for Newport.

Canton has been the home of many craftsmen. These are the tools used by the John family for their marquetry work during the restoration of Cardiff Castle (they are now housed in the Welsh Folk Museum at St Fagans).

Opposite: Gerry Parsons' great-grandfather was a founder-member of the Canton Corps of the Salvation Army, of which his grandfather and father were also life-long members. Gerry's own north-country accent comes from his parents' period of full-time work for the Army in Lancashire, where Gerry was born at Rochdale. After serving in the RAF, Gerry joined the Cardiff City Police force and became a desk-sergeant at Canton, where he also played the tuba in the Salvation Army band from 1952. He relishes the good stories that have come his way, including the one from the Canton desk telling of the 'dear old lady' who reported her cat lost. 'Go out and find her a cat', muttered the sergeant behind his hand to the junior, but he was overheard: 'Young man, don't you dare speak like that; I'll have you know mine was a special cat, a manx cat'. 'And chop off its tail', was the muttered response!

Acknowledgements

It has only been possible to begin to compile a history of Canton through the kindness and help of many people over the last ten years. Foremost among them have been Dr D.A. Bassett, Geoff Dart, Peter Bowen, the late Fred Jones, Dennis Pope, Miss Barbara Jones, Mr A.V. ('Vince') Jones and the late Mrs Beaty Jones, several of whom are members of the Local History Society. The expertise and assistance of the Cardiff Library Service (particularly that of the local studies librarian, Mr Brynmor Jones) has been invaluable, as has that of the Welsh Folk Museum (National Museum of Wales). The staff of Canton branch library have also been particularly helpful in the annual exhibitions of local history held since 1986, which were the genesis of this book. We are grateful to the Chalford Publishing Company for the opportunity to publish this book, and to their Wales editor, Mr Simon Eckley, for his considerate assistance.

This volume has only come about because so many people have cared for and shared their photographs. As many as possible of these are thanked here, together with those who have provided information, or help, in a variety of ways:

A. Ballinger; Peter Barry; Mr N. Billingham; Mr W.H. Bishop; Philip Biss (Chepstow); D.G. Bowen; John and Shirley Bowen-Humphreys; Mrs F. Burns; Brian Canning; Mr Walter Chick; Mr & Mrs Arthur Clark; Mrs G. Comer; County Record Office, Cardiff; Miss Barbara Davies (Penarth); Mrs M. Dodd; Mrs J. Dussman; Mr T.J. ('Tom') Evans; Mrs V.J. Ferisey; Mrs Audrey Fish; Mr Keith Flynn; Mrs Daphne Fullwood (Edinburgh); Dr John Gibbs (Penarth); Mrs B. Gibson; Mr K. Griffin; Mr & Mrs T. Grimshaw; Syd Gronow; Mrs N. Groves; Mr W.J. Harbourne; Mrs M. Harcom; Mrs D. Harding; John Harding; Mrs A. Hardy: Cliff Harris; Mrs Anne Harrison; R.M. Huish; Jean Hurley; Mr F.N. Jenkins; Mrs Betty King; Lloyds Private Banking Ltd, Novello House, Cathedral Road, Cardiff; Larry Lloyd; Mr K. Mathias; Mr G. North; Mrs A.M. O'Donovan; Miss Eileen Orpin; Mr G. Parsons; Mr Reg Paull; Nick Payne; Mrs A.M. Petty; Mr W. Penny; H.B. Priestley; Prontoprint (Canton branch); Terry Rees; Mrs E. Richards; N.S. Roberts; Ivor Rodway; Bjorn Simonsen; Mr & Mrs Alan Smith; Mr & Mrs E. Smith; Mr & Mrs R. Stuart; Chris Taylor; Revd & Mrs Haydn Thomas; Mrs Queenie Thomas; Mrs Yvonne Thomas; Mrs Alwyn Tyrrell; Mr T. Verallo; Mrs E. Walsh; Whitbread Archives; Mrs Betty Willis; Mr J. Worrell; Graham Williams; Matthew Williams; Miss Doreen Woodford; Much Wenlock; Mrs Shirley Wright. Also to Stewart Williams, publisher of *Cardiff Yesterday*, to whom we are indebted for encouraging us all to value and share our photographs. Apologies are given to anyone inadvertently omitted from the above list, who has helped me in this project, or in my previous local history work.

Finally, thank you to 'George' for his enthusiastic support.